More Praise for
Virtual Training Tools and Templates

"In these pages, you will catch some of Cindy Huggett's best ideas from her 15+ years of virtual expertise. She combines helpful tips, tools, and templates to help anyone jump into their next webinar!"

—Becky Pike Pluth
President and CEO, The Bob Pike Group

"This one resource will save you immeasurable numbers of hours creating your own tools and templates. Cindy Huggett's a bona fide authority, and I guarantee you'll learn something here. Don't make the mistakes all us old-timers have!"

—Roger Courville
Chief Content Officer, EventBuilder

"For most teams, getting started using virtual classrooms is the hardest part! There are hundreds of issues that need attention and the effort can seem intimidating, but *Virtual Training Tools and Templates* is illuminating. It will help you see clearly and do logically all the things that will have your virtual online training initiative make a great first impression—there's no need to start from scratch. If you want to run successful virtual classroom training events, have every team member and stakeholder read this book."

—Karen Hyder
Online Event Producer and Speaker Coach
Guild Master 2017

"Cindy Huggett is the virtual classroom guru. She knows the world of webinars, vILT, webcasts, and virtual classrooms like no one else, and has shared some of her wisdom with us in *Virtual Training Tools and Templates*. I love the hands-on approach she takes in this book to helping anyone interested in creating effective virtual training. I see this becoming an instructional designer's go-to guide for all things virtual."

—Treion Muller
Author, *The Webinar Manifesto* and *The Learning Explosion*,
Vice President, Digital Learning Solutions, TwentyEighty

☐ VIRTUAL
☐ TRAINING
☑ TOOLS AND
☐ TEMPLATES

An Action Guide to
Live Online Learning

CINDY
HUGGETT

atd
PRESS

22 21 20 19   2 3 4 5 6

All trademark attributions are listed at the end of the book. Some material and resources in this book appeared earlier in *The Virtual Training Guidebook: How to Design, Deliver, and Implement Live Online Training* (ASTD Press, 2013). Adobe Connect screenshots are reprinted with permission from Adobe Systems Incorporated.

ATD Press is an internationally renowned source of insightful and practical information on talent development, workplace learning, and professional development.

ATD Press
1640 King Street
Alexandria, VA 22314 USA

Ordering information: Books published by ATD Press can be purchased by visiting ATD's website at www.td.org/books or by calling 800.628.2783 or 703.683.8100.

Library of Congress Control Number: 2017941220
ISBN-10: 1-56286-575-7
ISBN-13: 978-1-56286-575-7
e-ISBN: 978-1-56286-576-4

ATD Press Editorial Staff
Director: Kristine Luecker
Manager: Melissa Jones
Community of Practice Manager, Learning Technologies: Justin Brusino
Developmental Editor: Kathryn Stafford
Senior Associate Editor: Caroline Coppel
Cover Design: Alban Fischer, Alban Fischer Design
Text Design: Francelyn Fernandez
Printed by Versa Press, Inc., East Peoria, IL

Contents

Introduction: My Journey in Virtual Training................................1

   1. Get Ready for Virtual Training...................................5

   2. Select Technology 37

   3. Design Content..61

   4. Develop Activities 93

   5. Work With Facilitators and Producers.........................123

   6. Prepare Participants 159

   7. Evaluate Results 183

Epilogue 207

References 213

List of Tools 215

Recommended Resources 219

Trademark Attributions 223

Acknowledgments 225

About the Author 227

Index...229

My Journey in Virtual Training

When I designed and facilitated my first virtual training class in the early 2000s, I did it out of necessity. I was a one-person training department in an organization that had employees scattered around the globe. I discovered that virtual training was an efficient way to reach my remote audience without having to get on an airplane. I could deliver learning programs from my home office while my audience learned from the comfort of their own desks.

At that time, there weren't any guides or how-to manuals, so I used a trial and error approach to figure out what worked. I took what I knew to be true about adult learning principles, combined it with my technology background as a Microsoft-certified software trainer, and jumped right in. I quickly learned that my virtual training programs needed to be fairly short, highly relevant, and extremely engaging. I also learned that smaller groups allowed for more interaction, and that it was important to get creative with the platform tools to encourage participation (Figure I-1).

Thankfully, my company's IT department had purchased an early version of WebEx to use for online meetings, and I was able to use its account for my training programs. I set up virtual classes on the platform and invited learners to join in. Unfortunately, we only had a license for five users at a time to be connected, so I regularly exceeded our allowance and had to pay overage fees. I had to figure out ways to partner with the IT team to make everything work. And I had to justify our extra investments to senior management for their approval and buy-in.

Does this sound familiar to you? Trying to figure out virtual training while having to partner with IT, working within constraints, and needing to persuade senior management to invest more in it?

One of my first online blended learning programs—a management development experience for frontline leaders—received mixed results. I designed a six-month program that included many distinct components: self-paced e-learning, live online virtual training sessions, and action assignments in between. The content itself was solid, but the structure needed help: I had made it too long and complicated, and had invited too many participants to go through at once. But it was a great learning experience for me! I took those lessons to heart and adjusted how I approached future blended and virtual designs.

Figure I-1. A Whiteboard Activity From One of Cindy's 2004 Virtual Training Classes

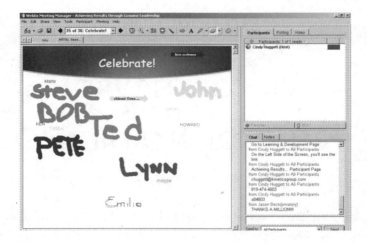

After leaving that organization in 2004 and striking out on my own, I continued to incorporate virtual training into the learning solutions I created for my clients. I started training other trainers how to transfer in-person facilitation skills to the online classroom. I helped my clients convert classroom programs to online ones. I taught individuals how to use various technology platforms. I consulted with organizations that were moving to the virtual classroom, offering advice and assistance with implementation strategies.

Fast forward to today, more than 15 years after that first virtual training class. I'm still using virtual training out of necessity to reach a global audience, but also because it's an effective way to learn. I'm still experimenting with creative techniques to use platform tools to engage participants. And I'm still learning new methods for designing, delivering, and implementing virtual training solutions.

Current Trends in Virtual Training

According to the Association for Talent Development's 2016 *State of the Industry* report, 42 percent of all learning delivered uses technology-based methods, up from 38 percent in previous years. Instructor-led live online training—what I call virtual training—is approximately 10 percent of all learning delivered. That's an almost 4 percent increase from five years ago, which is significant given the overall size of the industry.

Your organization is probably part of this trend—moving programs from the traditional face-to-face classroom to the online one. In fact, 86 percent of organizations either currently use or are planning to start using virtual classrooms soon (ATD 2017). So if you're like most, you're probably investigating ways to leverage technology, increase your reach to remote learners, create flexible learning programs, deliver better content in less time, and so on—all things that lend themselves well to virtual training. But you may be wondering if you're doing it in the most effective way possible, or if you can improve upon the results you're already seeing.

Those are all good questions to ponder as you survey the virtual training landscape. As the use of technology in training continues to rise, it's important to think carefully about how virtual training will help your employees be more productive and ultimately improve your business metrics.

About This Book

When my second book, *The Virtual Training Guidebook: How to Design, Deliver, and Implement Live Online Learning,* was published in 2013, I told several friends and colleagues that it was my "complete manifesto" on virtual training—my written guide to how virtual training could be interactive, engaging, and effective. It took a holistic approach to successful online learning by including information on implementation planning, selecting a platform, a three-step design model, trainer skills needed for virtual delivery, administrative and logistical considerations, and the importance of preparing participants for a successful learning experience. It included several ready-to-use checklists and "how-to" tips for organizations.

One of the consistent compliments I've received about that book is its practicality—that it's a resource designed to be used by practitioners in the field who need the nitty-gritty details and tools to get things done. My goal was to create a useful resource guide for L&D professionals.

However, over time I have realized that the book didn't go far enough. I had even more tools, templates, tips, and resources that would be helpful to organizations and individuals who want to successfully use virtual training. Also, over time, technology has changed, so several of my earlier checklists and templates have been updated. That's the big idea that motivated this book.

Virtual Training Tools and Templates is for anyone involved with virtual training, from instructional designers to facilitating trainers, learning coordinators to training managers. This book expands upon the ideas found in *The Virtual Training Guidebook* by offering a series of worksheets, checklists, templates, and tips for effective virtual training. Most of these resources are ones that I've created for my own work over the years, while others are supplemental materials that I've gathered from research or other experiences. A few of the tools appeared in my earlier books and are reintroduced here for convenience. Each chapter presents an introduction to place the subsequent resources in context.

In addition to the forms, tools, and templates that I use in my own virtual training projects, I've also asked many colleagues and clients to contribute. You'll hear their real-world experiences, lessons learned, and advice within these pages.

Here is a description of the chapters:

- **Chapter 1, Get Ready for Virtual Training,** begins by helping you prepare your organization for virtual training, with a four-step process for a successful launch.

This chapter also reviews the many definitions of virtual training, considers who should be involved in a virtual training rollout, and offers tools, tips, and templates for building a customized virtual training plan for your organization.

- **Chapter 2, Select Technology,** outlines the types of technology needed for successful virtual training implementations, including hardware, software, and other technology needed. It provides technology selection checklists and tips. It also looks at ways to work with IT departments on selecting technology and how to partner with suppliers.

- **Chapter 3, Design Content,** provides an overview of best practice virtual training design principles, reviews a three-step design process, and gives tips for converting traditional face-to-face courses to the online classroom. It also includes templates for creating facilitator and participant materials.

- **Chapter 4, Develop Activities,** focuses on how to create interactive virtual training sessions and includes activity planners, activity ideas, and guidelines for sequencing activities during an event. You'll also find tips to make webcasts and other online presentations more interactive.

- **Chapter 5, Work With Facilitators and Producers,** reviews the main roles needed for successful virtual delivery: facilitators and producers. It offers selection criteria for these roles along with the skills needed for success, and shows how to prepare them for delivering online. This chapter also contains preparation checklists, practice tips, and in-classroom techniques for creating an engaging learning environment.

- **Chapter 6, Prepare Participants,** provides tips and ideas for helping participants adjust to the virtual classroom and be successful—an often-overlooked component in virtual training programs. This chapter offers ways to teach learners the platform tools and ways to ensure they complete offline assignments, along with technology tips.

- **Chapter 7, Evaluate Results,** reviews how to evaluate the success of your virtual training in your organization. In addition to providing evaluation template samples, it gives after-action review templates and ways to collect evaluation data in a virtual training class.

Because the virtual training landscape will undoubtedly continue to grow and change in the future, I've also created a resource page on my website, www.cindyhuggett.com/actionguide, that will help us all stay current on trends. This resource page already includes some of the ready-to-use items found in this book, and serves as a go-to place for your questions and comments about virtual training. It also links to the ATD Press book landing page, where you'll find updates and additional resources. I hope to hear from you and learn from your virtual training experiences as well!

CHAPTER 1

Get Ready for Virtual Training

So you've decided to take the plunge into a virtual training initiative. Maybe you're trying to save money. Maybe you've heard about virtual training's many benefits. Perhaps your IT department purchased a web platform that everyone in the organization is using and you (the training department) want to use it, too. Or it could be that you have remote learners whom you haven't been able to reach with traditional programs, and virtual learning will extend that reach.

Regardless of your reason, this chapter will help you make the move to the virtual classroom. And if you've already begun virtual training in your organization, this chapter will help you make sure you've laid the proper foundation. It includes checklists and tools that will help you think through what your organization needs to do in four steps:

1. Get started.
2. Get ready.
3. Get buy-in.
4. Get going.

Also, whether you are planning a large-scale virtual training initiative or a small virtual program, you'll find useful templates in this chapter. I'll use the terms *initiative* and *program* interchangeably, because you can apply the resources to either scenario.

Get Started

Which comes first—the chicken or the egg? It's the age-old question without a definitive answer. Just like this question: Which comes first in a virtual training implementation—the design blueprint, the delivery plan, the administrative details, or something else? In reality, the fact that you're even asking or thinking about these questions indicates that you want to plan, and you're interested in doing it right and making sure that virtual training in your organization is the best it can be. So the answer to the question is yes! It's all important—design, delivery, and administration—regardless of the order in which you do things.

In implementing virtual training, the best place to start is with the end in the mind. Look at your end goal—what are you trying to achieve? Then work backward from there. As you determine your action plan—how to get from your current state to your future state—you'll map out the right implementation plan for your organization. For instance, I recently worked with two different clients. The end goal of one was to reduce travel costs while still offering training programs. The other client's end goal was to increase the reach of their training programs so they could eliminate a staffing bottleneck from not having enough programs to reach everyone who needed them. Both goals were the right targets for each organization and could be reached through a virtual training initiative.

The right implementation plan for your organization will depend on many factors. Virtual training plans and strategies typically include considerations for converting traditional classroom programs to virtual ones, information on selecting technology, guidance for upskilling facilitators, and plans to cover logistics. While your plan will be different from another organization's, all plans have some commonalities. Therefore, while this chapter may not have every detail that your project needs, the tools, forms, and templates found here will get you started on the journey and help you think through all the parts needed to start your virtual training initiative or program.

Get Ready

Before you jump into strategic planning, take a step back to make sure that virtual training is the right solution for your need. Virtual training has many benefits, yet it's not the answer to every problem.

For example, is your target audience remote, or are they all working under the same roof? Virtual training is best when the participants are remote—from the trainer and from one another. And, do the participants have the required technology—both in terms of equipment and Internet bandwidth—to make the virtual programs successful? How about the participant learning environments? Will they have a quiet place to learn, or will they try to join a session with their mobile device while driving down the road to get to the next client location? Also, is the topic appropriate for online learning? If the participants need hands-on experience with a piece of equipment and that equipment won't be available to them in the virtual classroom, does it make sense to offer virtual training for that content? These are just a few of the questions to consider as you determine if virtual training is right for your organization's needs.

Defining Virtual Training

Once you've determined that virtual training is the right solution, your next step is to define it. What does your organization mean by *virtual training*?

Over the past several years, I've asked thousands of people to share with me their definition of virtual training. And I've received almost as many different responses. One person thinks virtual training is a synchronous live online event, while someone else thinks virtual training is self-paced asynchronous learning, and another person thinks virtual training is a webcast that has one presenter and hundreds of attendees. One of my clients said they were going to "do virtual training," and by that they meant bringing tablets into the classroom for participant use during a face-to-face class.

Therefore, it's essential to define what you and your organization mean by virtual training. You might use more than one type of virtual training, such as holding presentation-style webcasts for awareness and small group virtual training classes for skill-building. Or you might decide that all your virtual programs will be called "classes," will be exactly 45 minutes long, and allow no more than 20 people each. Or you might do something else altogether. What's critical is that you define it, and make sure everyone in your organization is on the same page.

Webinars, Webcasts, and Virtual Training

What's the difference between a webcast, a webinar, and a virtual training class? The amount of participant interactivity and the number of participants (Figure 1-1). Webcasts have the largest audience with the least amount of interactivity, then webinars, and then virtual training classes.

Figure 1-1. Comparing Webcasts, Webinars, and Virtual Training

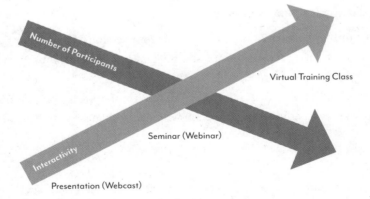

Whether you plan to have a one-way presentation, a panel discussion, a facilitated meeting, or an interactive virtual training class, you can use many of the tools in this chapter to plan your online initiative.

It's important to think through your definition, because it will guide your entire strategy. Maybe all you plan to do is schedule informative webcasts that share new product features with your entire large sales population. Or, maybe your goal is to host open-registration lunch & learn–style webinars on various topics for educational purposes. Or, maybe your target is to assimilate new hires into the company culture by offering a virtual orientation program for small groups of employees. Or perhaps you want to offer leadership development topics for high-potential directors advancing into executive management roles. Each one of these scenarios represents different types of virtual training. And each one would call for a different strategy and implementation plan. Therefore, I can't stress enough how imperative it is that you begin by defining what virtual training means in your organization.

Here's my definition of virtual training: *a highly interactive, synchronous online, instructor-led training class, with defined learning objectives, that has geographically dispersed participants, each one individually connected using a web classroom platform.*

Notice the key words:

- **highly interactive:** participants engage frequently, at least every few minutes, with the facilitator, learning content, and virtual classroom tools

- **synchronous online:** participants meet at the same time; sometimes referred to as live or, in the case of virtual training, live online

- **instructor-led:** facilitated by a professional trainer or facilitator

- **defined learning objectives:** clearly stated performance expectations that learners will be able to achieve as a result of actively participating in the session

- **geographically dispersed:** learners are distributed and apart from one another, not in the same room

- **individually connected:** all participants join from their own devices and have their own audio or telephone connection

- **web classroom platform:** a training or classroom version of a software program that allows for online screen and file sharing and has audience interaction tools such as polling, chatting, and breakouts.

It's OK if your definition of virtual training is different from mine, as long as you have taken the time to define what you and your organization will mean when you say "virtual training."

Get Buy-In

Virtual training plans are rarely created in isolation. Just as it takes a village to get things done in most organizations, it takes a team to create successful virtual training. This cadre of supporters should work together on the implementation.

Therefore, one of the first steps will be to identify the team who will help you define and implement your virtual training strategy. These are your stakeholders—anyone who has a stake in the virtual training program. Executives who fund the training, facilitators who deliver the training, designers who create the training, internal employees or external clients who attend the training—all of these roles would be considered stakeholders.

> **In Action: Advice From Jack Benedict, Manager of Process and Quality, Volvo Trucks**
>
> In 2013, Volvo Trucks started implementing virtual training. Jack Benedict and others in the learning department looked at the number of customers they needed to reach (450 locations across seven time zones) versus the training resources they had, and decided to explore online solutions.
>
> Jack and the team started with the question, "What would we tell them if we only had one hour? What are the key things that the learners could apply immediately?" They were looking for the most efficient way to deliver the most important concepts and landed on virtual training as the answer.
>
> They began to define virtual training—what it is and what it isn't—and created a set of design principles to follow. They also began searching for a platform that had robust features yet would be easy for learners to use. And they began building the business case to gain buy-in and acceptance throughout the organization.
>
> Jack's advice to others who are getting started with virtual training? He boils it down to three main things:
>
> 1. Define a very small target for the initial virtual training implementation. Start with a simple topic and small audience that will have a large impact on results. You can be forward thinking as a learning organization, but because change makes many people nervous, start small for success.
>
> 2. Define what virtual training is, and what it means to your organization. Document the definition and gain acceptance of it, so that it becomes your guidepost for design, delivery, and implementation.
>
> 3. Define what tools you need for virtual training, then select a platform that has those tools. Also, make sure that your organizational infrastructure can handle the platform so that people don't get frustrated by the technology.

Once you identify them, you may need to employ change management techniques to gain their initial support. If anyone is unwilling to join in the discussion, consider sharing the many benefits of virtual training and how it could help the organization achieve a particular goal. Present your case in a way that appeals to them, such as saying something like, "You can save time by not having to travel to attend your next training program."

Get Going

Now that you've identified virtual training as a solution, you've defined what virtual training means to your organization, and you've determined the stakeholders, it's time to create the strategy. (You can also define virtual training as part of your strategy instead of before it.)

Your strategic plan might be a one-page goal-setting document or an elaborate implementation plan. In project management circles, the implementation plan is often referred to as the project charter, so you might even call it that. It will outline the scope and definition of your virtual training initiative, establish stakeholder buy-in, and provide an implementation framework. Remember, your initial plan will be unique to your situation.

Tips, Tools, and Templates

To help you get ready for virtual training, here are the tools and templates that will enable you to think through strategy and implementation planning. They will give you a head start on creating a path forward for your organization's virtual training initiatives.

Tool 1-1. A Thought-Starter: Is Virtual Training the Right Solution?

To help determine if virtual training is the correct solution to use for your organization, consider the following questions.

- **Are the participants centrally located or dispersed?** If your organization is not going to save on travel expenses because everyone is in the same location, then consider sticking with in-person training. It may be just as fast for them to walk down the hallway to your training room as it would be for them to log in to a virtual classroom.

- **What technology barriers affect success?** Participants and facilitators need to have the appropriate technology available to them. The exact technology needed will vary depending upon the virtual software program used; however, a typical technology setup requires a high-speed Internet connection, a sound card and speakers to hear streaming media, a phone or voice over Internet Protocol (VoIP) capabilities, and administrative privileges to install software.

- **Do you have qualified trainers and producers to facilitate the virtual training event?** Classroom trainers need a new skill set to effectively deliver virtual training. They need to be comfortable with technology, able to multitask well, and know how to engage participants whom they can't see. These skills come with training and practice; however, this trainer preparation time should be factored into the decision. In addition, a virtual training event will go much smoother if a producer is involved with the facilitation. The producer is a second person who assists the trainer with technology, troubleshooting, and running the virtual event, and helps create a seamless experience for participants. Is your existing training staff large enough to support facilitators and producers for virtual events? If not, can a budget be secured to add staff or to outsource this capability?

- **Will every participant and facilitator have an appropriate learning environment?** Participants and facilitators need to have their own computer connection and telephone line to attend the virtual event. They should be in a quiet area conducive to learning. If they are in an open space or cubicle environment, they will need headphones or another way to tune out external noise.

- **Who will administer the logistical details for the training program?** The online environment creates a long list of logistics that need to be executed for a successful class. This includes creating the virtual classroom events within the software's administrative tools, getting links and passwords to everyone who needs them, distributing handouts and other class materials to participants, and helping participants troubleshoot technical problems prior to class.

- **Do all participants speak the same language?** Virtual training can be an excellent way to provide training to an international population, as long as language barriers do not get in the way.

Tool 1-2. Organizational Analysis Tool

Use this big-picture questionnaire to start thinking about virtual training and its potential as a solution in your organization. Note that you may need to adjust some of the questions to fit your organization. For example, you might need to focus on just one business unit instead of the entire organization, or you might need to narrow the scope to a subset of training programs.

1. What are your organization's key indicators of success? What's measured? How is it measured? (For example, revenue targets, cost adherence, customer satisfaction, and products shipped.)

2. What factors contribute to these metrics?

3. What organizational initiatives currently exist to satisfy these metrics, such as sales incentives, quality improvement programs, and workplace safety goals?

4. Which roles in the organization directly affect these metrics? Which roles indirectly affect them? For example, call center customer service reps might directly affect first-call resolution metrics, but the back office support team also indirectly influences these metrics.

5. What knowledge and skills are needed to influence or affect these metrics?

6. What training programs already exist to address necessary knowledge and skills? How are they currently delivered?

7. Which of these training programs are a good fit for virtual delivery?

8. Which programs are missing? Could or should they be added?

9. What are the demographics of your learner population or target audience?

    a. Are they centrally located or dispersed?

    b. Are they tech savvy or tech novices?

    c. Do they have necessary hardware, software, and bandwidth?

    d. Are they already familiar with online learning?

10. What other factors are important to know about them?

11. Given all the previous information, what is the path forward for your organization regarding virtual training?

Tool 1-3. Goal-Planning Worksheet

Begin with a clear idea of the results you want to achieve when setting goals for your virtual training initiatives. Goal planning is important whether you have a single virtual program or an extensive series of virtual classes. To help you set effective goals, consider the questions on this planning worksheet.

1. What's the big goal for your virtual training program or initiative? What specifically do you hope to accomplish?

2. What do participants need to do as a result of this training program?
   - ❏ Be more knowledgeable about the topic.
   - ❏ Behave differently.
   - ❏ Take action on something.
   - ❏ Other:

3. How will the organization change or improve as a result?

4. What's the best way to achieve the aforementioned goals?

5. How specifically will virtual training help achieve these outcomes?

Tool 1-4. Brainstorming for Success Worksheet

Sometimes a blank page is the best way to envision a goal. Use this brainstorming worksheet to sketch out your vision for success, then use it as a springboard for developing more detailed goals and project planning.

Tool 1-5. Benefits Checklist: Which Will You Realize?

By implementing virtual training in your organization, what benefits will you realize? Select from the list below, and then use these items in your discussions with key stakeholders.

❐ Better transfer of knowledge to learners

❐ Gain competitive advantage

❐ Positive effect on specific business results

❐ Reach a previously isolated audience (expanded reach of training programs)

❐ Add flexibility to your program offerings

❐ Opportunities for dispersed learners to interact and network with one another

❐ Increase workforce productivity

❐ Reduced costs (compared with in-person training programs) in areas such as:
   - travel costs for participants
   - travel costs for trainers
   - time away from office.

❐ Other:

❐ Other:

❐ Other:

Tool 1-6. Virtual Training Definition Brainstorm

How will your organization define virtual training? You may end up creating several different definitions, and then choosing the appropriate one for each event. Consider the following factors and circle your choice for each one.

- **Audience Size**
  Large (more than 50)   Medium (25-50)   Small (5-24)

- **Delivery Style**
  Presentation   Facilitation

- **Learning Objectives**
  Do not have learning objectives   Have learning objectives

- **Content**
  Information dissemination   Skill building

The more circles you have on the left, the more "presentation-only, webcast-style" your online events will be.

Tool 1-7. Virtual Training Definition Documents

An organization's virtual training definition document is created to establish a common understanding among all internal stakeholders (instructional designers, trainers, and other members of the organization's learning department) around virtual training. It's not a one-size-fits-all definition document. In some organizations, a short one-paragraph description will suffice. In other organizations, a detailed list would be appropriate. I have provided two very different samples below to spur your thinking about virtual training in your organization.

Sample 1: Virtual Training Definition Document

This organization uses a simple, one-sentence definition.

> Virtual training is a live, facilitated training class that uses technology to connect learners to one another. It's a highly engaging and interactive learning experience.

Sample 2: Virtual Training Definition Document

This organization created a lengthy definition and included descriptions of what it is and is not.

Our Organization's Virtual Training Definition and Principles

Our goal for virtual training is the rapid design and delivery of targeted content to appropriate audiences.

What It Is

- Highly interactive
- Live
- Facilitated
- Synchronous

It uses a virtual classroom platform to enable geographically separated learners and facilitators to interact with one another. It has at least one defined learning objective and a measurable learning outcome.

What It Is Not

- It is not a webinar, or online meeting, which is predominantly one-way communication from a presenter to a large group with minimal opportunities to interact.
- It is not asynchronous learning, in which an individual participant uses a computer to acquire knowledge from the content without interacting with others.
- It is not a distance learning session, in which the leader is in one location and connects with a group of participants in another location using video- or audioconferencing.
- It is not a live session recorded for playback and viewed as a video for future consumption.
- It will not replace in-person, instructor-led training, in which hands-on practice is essential.

Our Guidelines

- Virtual training sessions will be scheduled for 60 minutes; however, they will be designed to last no more than 45 minutes.

- Each session will have one key learning objective, and typically no more than two objectives.

- To minimize distractions or learners disengaging to multitask, virtual training sessions will require interaction at least every three to five minutes.

- Activities will be both meaningful and relevant (that is, we don't ask participants to answer a poll just to take a poll).

- Sessions will take advantage of the full set of the web platform's tools, including chats, polls, whiteboards, small group activities, and breakout rooms. These features will be leveraged to create an interactive learning experience for participants.

- To help keep participant interest, onscreen visuals must change at least every one and a half to two minutes. Visuals include slides, annotations, or other items that could appear onscreen.

- If materials external to the live online class are needed during the session, participants must be able to print them.

- Participants need individual interaction to support learning, engagement, and live skills practice. As a result, virtual training class sizes will be kept small, to no more than 20 participants a session. In addition, all participants will connect individually, using their computer or laptop and audio connection.

- Participants will connect to sessions through their computer or laptop, not mobile devices. For the foreseeable future, mobile device apps will not be supported.

- Sessions will be led by one trained facilitator. The facilitator will have administrative technical support for at least the beginning of each session.

- Virtual trainers will be trained to function in a virtual training environment. They will be carefully selected and prepared for effective virtual delivery.

- Because the success of virtual training depends on live interaction and engagement, sessions will not be recorded for playback, except in rare instances when extenuating circumstances warrant it. Participants will need to attend the live session.

- Participants unable to attend a live session will be rescheduled for a future session or directed to other learning resources.

Virtual Training Definition Document Worksheet

Use this definition document to help define virtual training in your organization.

Virtual training is:

Virtual training is not:

Our guidelines and ground rules for virtual training:

Tool 1-8. Stakeholder Identification Checklist

Who should be involved with your virtual training implementation? Probably more people than you think. Use the following table to help you define stakeholders in your organization and select from the roles and descriptions shown. Note that each role listed may not be a specific job title. Instead, they are job functions that carry out responsibilities that affect the success of virtual training. Also, in some organizations, one person may play more than one role. For example, the instructor who delivers virtual training may also be the person who designed it. The smaller the organization, the more likely one person will have multiple roles. And on the flip side, there may be more than one person for each function, such as IT representatives for each location.

Role	Description	Your Organization
Executive Sponsors	The senior executives who can support and champion the virtual training initiative at the highest levels of the organization.	
Resource Owners	Those who control resources needed for creating, designing, delivering, and implementing virtual training. This could be training management, procurement officers, IT managers, or other managers who control budget and other needed resources.	
Content Owners	Subject matter experts who have deep knowledge of the training topic. They might be an employee in the field, or a manager with responsibility for the subject matter. They can help design the training and ensure topic relevancy.	
Designers	Instructional designers who create the virtual training program or convert classroom programs to online ones. This role might include graphic designers as well as professionals who specialize in adult learning methodologies and instructional technology.	

Role	Description	Your Organization
Facilitators	The people in front of the class who deliver the training sessions; also called "trainers" or "instructors."	
Producers	Technical experts who assist the facilitators during live online sessions. Some producers specialize in technology-only assistance (working with participants who need help connecting), while other producers co-facilitate sessions along with the trainer. In some cases, a producer may be called a "host" or "moderator."	
Coordinators	The administrative people who handle logistical details of virtual training events. They might also administer the organization's learning management system and communicate with participants before and after an event.	
Technicians	Usually called IT (information technology) or IS (information services), they own the technology—both hardware and software—needed for virtual training success. These roles also include the owner or admin of the organization's learning management system.	
Participants	Participants are also known as learners or program attendees. Because they are the ultimate customer of the virtual training initiative, include a representative sample in the initial planning stages.	
Managers	As the participants' managers, they need to support the full participation of their employees. This group's buy-in is critical to success because they will allow participants time to attend training, as well as reinforce the skills learned.	

Tool 1-9. Virtual Training Budget Template

Virtual training isn't free. Just because it's online and makes use of technology doesn't mean that it's without cost. A virtual training class may be less expensive than its in-person counterpart, and over time it may help reach more learners at less cost. But it takes resources to get to that point. There are many initial up-front investments to make and ongoing costs to maintain the program. Use this simplified budget template to help estimate the initial and ongoing investments.

Category	Line Item	Detail	Estimated Amount
Initial Costs			
	Web-based classroom platform	Setup fees and implementation costs	
	Hardware	Including facilitator needs, such as laptops or headsets	
	Training and education for employees	Costs to upskill designers, facilitators, and producers	
	Instructional design fees	Costs to create virtual training classes	
	LMS upgrade to integrate with web platform, if applicable	If you have an LMS, this cost would apply	
	Other:		
Ongoing Costs			
	Web-based classroom platform	Annual subscription fees	
	Per-event teleconference fees*	Include both domestic and international rates for global audiences	
	Salary and benefits (or contracting fees) for virtual training staff		
	Other:		

*If you choose to use VoIP audio instead of teleconferencing, then you may need to substitute increased Internet bandwidth for this line item.

Tool 1-10. Benefit-Cost Analysis Worksheet

If you need to justify a virtual training implementation, consider the following benefit-cost analysis. Select the items that apply to your situation, add estimated monetary values to each, total each column, and then complete the calculation shown.

Potential Increased Costs
(Compared With Traditional Classroom Training)

Item	Estimated Amount (+/-)
☐ Virtual classroom software platform subscription for administrators, trainers, and producers	
☐ Integrated telephone or conference call subscription and per-event costs (if not using VoIP)	
☐ Computer hardware needs, such as hands-free telephone headsets for participants	
☐ Higher printing costs for learners, who are often asked to print their own materials	
☐ Two facilitators, or a facilitator and a producer, for each virtual event	
☐ A second laptop for trainers who need to be logged in to the platform twice (once as a presenter and once as a participant)	
☐ Training for staff (designers and trainers) who need to learn the new virtual classroom software platform and how to design and deliver virtual training	
☐ Design and development time for the training curriculum*	
☐ LMS: Need to purchase additional integration for the web platform	
☐ Other:	
☐ Other:	
Total:	

*It takes an average of 43 hours of development time to create one hour of instructor-led training, and between 48 and 49 hours of development time to create one hour of interactive virtual training (Kapp and Defelice 2009).

Potential Decreased Costs
(Compared With Traditional Classroom Training)

Item	Estimated Amount (+/-)
❑ Reduced travel fees for both participants and trainers	
❑ Classroom materials that no longer need to be purchased (chart paper, markers, etc.)	
❑ Printing costs of classroom materials	
❑ Regain productivity time with participants not leaving their desk to attend training in another location	
❑ Other:	
❑ Other:	
Total:	

Benefit-Cost Analysis Calculation

Benefits Realized From Virtual Training – Cost to Implement Virtual Training =

_____ – _____ = _____

Budget Lesson Learned

A large global organization implemented virtual training. While many things about the programs were going well, in almost every class, numerous participants struggled with technical challenges. For example, they heard "choppy" audio or lost connectivity to the session. It was not an effective learning experience for those participants.

The root cause was finally identified as lack of sufficient bandwidth. The training team had chosen to rely on VoIP for audio to keep costs to a minimum, yet they didn't account for unreliable Internet bandwidth speeds. They had to revise their budget to include teleconferencing fees and increased bandwidth for several of their office locations. It was a budget lesson learned.

Tool 1-11. Building the Business Case

Your virtual training initiative should be in response to a business problem or challenge. Better yet, it could be a proactive solution to an anticipated challenge or an opportunity to positively influence business results. Either way, the program you develop should be in tune with the business. To do this, you'll need to keep abreast of the organization's key indicators and new initiatives.

The business case for virtual training should be presented to whoever controls the needed resources and has the authority to share them. All or some of the business case might also be presented to key stakeholders to help them see the benefits of virtual training.

In some cases, you won't need to create a business case for an entire virtual training initiative, but instead will simply need to justify a larger-than-planned investment in technology, or advocate for purchasing a specific platform that has a unique feature. Or you might only need to gain a stakeholder's verbal support and commitment. Whatever your need, use the following tool to help think through and plan your business case.

1. What is the request you want? Be specific. It could be tangible or intangible.

2. Whose support do you need for your request?

3. What business problems will virtual training help solve? Or, what business opportunities will be realized? How so?

4. How is information from question 3 relevant to your stakeholders (people listed in question 2)? What will be of most interest to them?

5. What specific resources will be needed from the stakeholders? Time? Money? Other?

6. What's the best communication method to reach the stakeholders?
    - ❒ In-person meeting
    - ❒ Conference call
    - ❒ Email
    - ❒ Text
    - ❒ Other:

7. What information will you share, and in what format?

8. What else is important to consider as you plan to present the business case?

Building a Business Case for Virtual Training at NTSB

The National Transportation Safety Board (NTSB) is a small government agency that realized that virtual training could help it expand its education offerings. Cindy Keegan, technical training officer at the NTSB Training Center, was tasked with setting up the virtual training program. She wanted to ensure that is was fully prepared for a successful implementation, so she began researching all the options available.

Cindy started by pulling together an internal team to explore virtual training options. I consulted with this team to help them think through a potential virtual training strategy. We spent time exploring the definition of virtual training at NTSB, the types of programs that would work well online, the various platforms that could be used, and the technology needed for success.

The team then built the business case for virtual training. Cindy put together a presentation that outlined the strategy, requirements, and benefits. "We did a great job of convincing our management that virtual training was the way to go," she said.

The team wanted to test out and pilot some virtual training before they made final decisions, so they hired a supplier that had its own courses, facilitators, and platform. This step helped the NTSB experience some virtual training classes without a long-term commitment.

"It was a good lesson learned," said Cindy. "We learned about some bandwidth issues, and we were able to collect feedback from our learners. It helped us know what we needed to do. We'll be using this information to move forward in our implementation planning. I've now put together a business case for increasing our Internet bandwidth, and we'll be selecting a platform soon."

Tool 1-12. Strategy Planning Meeting

When I'm working with clients to begin a virtual training strategic planning process, I'll invite all the stakeholders to a one-day meeting. We use this meeting for a high-level review of all aspects of the virtual training initiative. My goal is to facilitate discussion and generate thinking so that a project charter or an implementation plan can be created. The following is a typical agenda that we follow.

Planning Meeting Sample Agenda

Estimated Time*	Topic	Details and Sample Discussion Questions
9-9:30 a.m.	Welcome and overview: introductions, expectations, and administrative	Make sure everyone knows one another. Confirm agenda and set expectations for the meeting. Review administrative logistics.
9:30-10:45 a.m.	Defining virtual training	Discuss the different types of virtual training (webcasts, webinars, classes) and where virtual training fits in the organization. What's the vision for success? What business challenges will it help solve?
10:45-11 a.m.	Break	
11 a.m.–12 p.m.	Design considerations (engagement and transfer)	Which training programs should be converted to or created as virtual? Who will design and develop these programs? What design methodology will you follow? How will the designs support learner engagement? How will the designers be upskilled in virtual training? How will learning transfer be measured?
12-1 p.m.	Lunch	
1-2 p.m.	Delivery considerations (readiness and education)	Who will facilitate the programs? What roles will they play, such as facilitators, co-facilitators, and producers? How will the facilitators be upskilled in virtual training? How will they learn the platform features? What materials will you provide? How much preparation time will they have? What continuous improvement methods will you employ for their ongoing development?
2:45-3 p.m.	Break	

Estimated Time*	Topic	Details and Sample Discussion Questions
3-4 p.m.	Administration (technology and logistics)	Which web classroom platform should be used? Which suppliers should be or will be considered? Who will administer the accounts? Who will have ownership of this technology? Who will distribute information to facilitators for delivery, and to participants for programs? How will program materials get to participants? If an LMS is used, how will it be integrated? Will mobile devices be supported? What other technology or logistic items need to be reviewed?
4-4:15 p.m.	Review, revisit remaining questions	
4:15-4:30 p.m.	Wrap-up and next steps	

*Times are approximate and may change depending upon conversation flow.

Meeting Attendees:

- representatives from all stakeholder categories

Meeting Outcomes:

- increased awareness of virtual training implementation considerations
- creation of a draft virtual training strategy document (team charter or implementation plan)

Planning Meeting Agenda Template
Use this agenda template to plan your strategy meeting.

Estimated Time	Topic	Details and Sample Discussion Questions

Meeting Attendees:

-
-
-

Meeting Outcomes:

-
-
-

Virtual Training Project Meeting Minutes and Action Items Template

Use this template to track your virtual training meeting minutes and corresponding action items.

Action Item	Owner	Due Date

Tool 1-13. Virtual Training Project Team Charter and Strategy Template

As your virtual training initiative gets going, it's helpful to have a team charter that clearly states the mission and purpose of your project, the roles each person will play, the tasks that need to occur, and any risks or obstacles that could hinder success. This project charter could also serve as the basis of your project implementation plan.

Our Team's Target: We will do _____ by _____.

Major Milestones to Reach the Target

Milestone	Due Date

Tasks That Need to Happen to Reach the Target

Task and Sub-Task	Owner	Resources Needed	Due Date

Approvals Needed

Item That Needs Approval	By Whom?

Communication Methods

How Will We Communicate?	How Often?

Risks Identified

Potential Risks and Roadblocks	Severity (High, Medium, Low)	Action to Take

Other Key Items to Note

Tool 1-14. RACI Model

The RACI model (sometimes called RASCI) is a commonly used tool to identify roles and responsibilities on a project team. The RACI model has its roots in project management techniques. Each letter in the acronym refers to a level of ownership and decision-making authority. *R*, "responsibility," is usually the person assigned a task. *A*, "accountable," is the person who ultimately owns the task. *C*, "consulted," refers to the person who provides input for the tasks because of subject matter expertise or other necessary information. *I*, "informed," is the person or people who need to be kept informed on the items. If *S*, "support," is used, it refers to anyone who supports the task.

To fill in the RACI model, list the major tasks in the first column. Then list the project team members and other relevant stakeholders across the top. (Add more columns and rows if necessary.) For each task, identify who is accountable and who is responsible. Then fill in the other slots as needed.

Task	Name 1	Name 2	Name 3	Name 4
Investigate Platforms	*Melissa (C)*	*Christian (R)*	*Maria (I)*	*Alex (A)*

Summary

The virtual training planning process will naturally include implementation plans for selecting technology, creating designs, delivering sessions, and coordinating administrative logistics. You'll find the tools and templates needed for those throughout the rest of the book, starting with the next chapter.

CHAPTER 2

Select Technology

Technology decisions rise to the top of the list when it comes to virtual training implementations. The specific platform used to deliver virtual training plays a key role in its success. The hardware components that facilitators and learners use with the platform also matter. In addition, audio quality—whether it be voice over Internet Protocol (VoIP) or integrated telephony—makes a huge difference in the overall learning experience.

There are so many choices available on the market that it can be difficult to decide which platform to choose for your virtual training initiative. What audio options will be best for your programs? What hardware components do you need to purchase? How much Internet bandwidth do you need?

If you're like many training professionals, and me when I first started on my virtual training journey more than 15 years ago, you'll go with whatever the IT department has purchased for the organization. Employees have company-issued devices, with pre-authorized software programs already installed and office-Internet connections already established, so the choice seems final. But are those "official" items really the best option for your virtual training programs? It's worth doing some due diligence to make the right decision.

For example, your organization's online collaboration program that allows employees to instant message one another also has document sharing, whiteboard, and polling features. Does that mean you should use this software for virtual training? It may or may not be the right choice. The whiteboard and polling features make it seem similar to a virtual classroom platform; however, the limited availability of training features (like breakout groups) might not be enough to create the learning environment you need.

Or you might be like another organization that purchased a platform for its global virtual training rollout, but didn't take into account the limited Internet bandwidth at some remote locations or plan to include a teleconference option for audio connections. Its virtual training program immediately experienced challenges.

So before considering your technology choices, let's briefly review the four key technology areas that every organization should consider when preparing for virtual training: hardware, software, audio, and Internet bandwidth. Each item requires careful attention because each affects the quality and cost of your virtual training.

Hardware

The first item each participant needs for virtual training success is a computer with a reliable Internet connection. It could be a laptop or a desktop computer of any make, model, or brand, provided that it meets the stated requirements of the web classroom platform you choose (that is, you'll need X amount of memory, minimum Internet connection speed of Y, and enough hardware space for any necessary software downloads).

According to my definition of virtual training, all participants should have their own computer connection. If you work in an organization that does not supply computers to each person (such as retail employees, construction workers, or manufacturing operators), then you'll need to make arrangements for them to have access. This could be a shared computer in a quiet location that individuals go to when it's their turn to participate in a virtual event.

Note that the most effective virtual facilitators use two computers when delivering training. This is so they can view the host screen as well as the participant view, which allows them to keep an eye on what participants see. It's also so they have a backup computer in case of technology failure or another unexpected situation. This is especially important if the facilitator is working solo, without a co-presenter or producer.

Mobile Devices

Most Americans—95 percent—own a cell phone; 77 percent own a smartphone, a 42 percent increase in only six years (Pew Research Center 2017). This trend is replicated all over the globe, with Cisco (2016) calculating that smart mobile devices will also increase exponentially in the coming years. Because more people are purchasing and using mobile devices than ever before, you might wonder why you shouldn't just use mobile devices in lieu of a computer or laptop for virtual training. They are usually cheaper to purchase than a laptop, and many users already own devices that they can (and do) use for work.

Here's what I wrote in 2013, in *The Virtual Training Guidebook:*

> Mobile devices can be used to connect to most online meetings and virtual events. Most virtual classroom software platforms have apps that correlate to their online programs. However, they work best in situations where participation remains passive—such as a webcast—because the controls are still often not as robust as the full version available on computers.
>
> The limitations of mobile apps for virtual training are rapidly diminishing, and will most likely not be an issue at some point in the future. Mobile apps will update, software platforms will evolve, and features will become seamless.

Unfortunately, even after several years, the situation is still the same. There are mobile apps for nearly every virtual classroom platform. Yet most of them still have limited functionality.

Participants on mobile devices do not typically have access to the full scope of tools and features available in the desktop versions.

For example, in one popular program, the mobile app doesn't let participants answer poll questions. And in another, the mobile app doesn't show video playback. Some virtual classroom apps don't let participants write on the whiteboard. If these features are used in virtual training activities as they usually are, then the mobile user experience would be quite different from the laptop user experience—and learning transfer would be compromised. Figures 2-1 and 2-2 compare one platform's mobile and desktop versions.

Figure 2-1. Adobe Connect Mobile

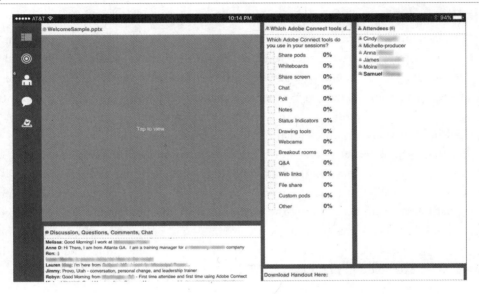

Figure 2-2. Adobe Connect Desktop

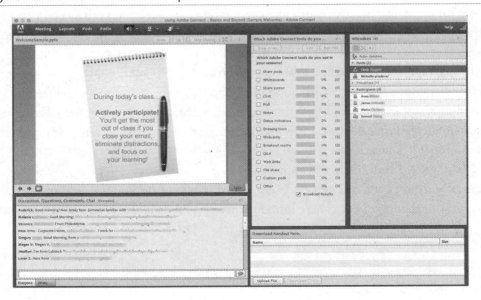

Another issue with mobile devices is making sure there is a stable Internet connection with enough data and bandwidth to handle the virtual class activities. Participants who use mobile devices need to find reliable wireless networks, or they need a data plan capable of supporting the virtual class.

While using mobile devices for virtual training will most certainly become common in the future, for now, the limited functionality of mobile virtual classroom apps still creates challenges. I do not recommend using them unless the virtual training program is specifically designed to only use available mobile features. I hope this will change soon as the apps become more sophisticated.

Headsets

Participants, facilitators, and producers—in fact, anyone who attends virtual training classes—should have a headset. Otherwise, they will need to uncomfortably cradle a phone on their shoulder, while typing and frequently engaging in the platform. Or they'll have to use a speakerphone, which can be hard to hear, give off echoes, pick up extra noises, and become disruptive to the class. Participants who use speakerphones may also distract their office mates.

A wired headset is also recommended to ensure crystal-clear sound. The other option—a wireless headset—sometimes encounters interference, which can be distracting to the user. The static can also sometimes be heard on the conference line, which becomes distracting to the class.

Scott King, co-founder of ReadyTalk, wrote in a 2014 blog post that "audio quality is the most important element in determining the success of an online conference. . . . Typically, the brain reacts to the loudest source of input. Any combination of poor volume, background noise, line static, echo, distortions, and other impairments can be introduced simultaneously, causing the brain to work extra hard to find focus."

Webcams

If you plan for facilitators or participants to see one another on video, then you'll need webcams. The webcams could be built into the laptop or desktop video monitor, or be a separate piece of equipment that captures streaming video in the platform.

Many years ago, I thought webcams should not be used at all. Having a webcam on the facilitator's face in a virtual training class put too much focus on this person as a presenter, and not enough emphasis on the learners. I have since softened this stance for a few reasons. First, many virtual classroom platforms now allow everyone to turn on their webcam, and all participants can be seen at once. (Of course, this is assuming you have a relatively small class size!) Second, video quality has improved since then, and learners are more accustomed to seeing a speaker's face when she talks. Third, I still recommend that a virtual facilitator turn on the webcam for a few minutes at the beginning of a session to introduce herself, and then turn it off for the remainder of the time. As long as the use of webcams enhances the participant experience (rather than detracting from it), then they can be a good addition to a virtual training event.

Software

The key software needed for a virtual training initiative is the virtual classroom platform. Sometimes it's called a web conferencing program, an online collaboration platform, or virtual meeting software. I typically refer to it as the virtual classroom software program or the virtual classroom platform.

Virtual Classroom Platforms

These platforms contain a variety of features that are used for group collaboration and inter-activity. For example, facilitators can ask questions through a poll, or by asking participants to respond in chat. Whiteboards allow for group brainstorming. Status indicators let participants respond to yes or no questions or raise their hands. And breakouts let smaller groups of participants get together for role plays or team discussions. For a description of the most common platform tools, there's a list in Tool 2-3 at the end of the chapter.

It's important to note that most virtual classroom software programs are part of a suite of similar products offered by a supplier. For example, Cisco WebEx has four products: Event Center, Meeting Center, Training Center, and Support Center. And there is Citrix GoTo-Meeting, GoToTraining, and GoToWebinar. This is important because each product includes different features. For instance, one product might have public chat, while another product from the same supplier might only allow for private chat.

Organizations should use the training or classroom version of a supplier's product for virtual training classes. It simply makes sense that a training product be used for organizational learning. It also provides the most robust, interactive tools that learners need to stay completely engaged in the learning experience. While it's possible to use a meeting or webinar product for virtual training, it's usually not the best alternative. Tool 2-4 reviews the key differences between meeting, training, and webinar programs.

Other Programs

There may also be other software programs that are needed for your organization's overall online training strategy and, therefore, intersect with the virtual training platform. One of these is a learning management system (LMS) or other database that tracks organizational learning. An LMS can automate many of the administrative processes that surround virtual training. It can communicate with virtual training platforms, be the registration engine for participants, and send out automated reminders for events. The tools and templates section of this chapter offers tips for integrating virtual classroom platforms with an LMS.

When virtual training is a component of a blended learning solution, another helpful program is an online portal. This could be an internal discussion board or social media platform, or some other online collaboration tool. This type of system helps create a community among the participants of a blended curriculum, giving them a place and space to communicate with one another between live events. These online spaces may also offer document storage for offline activity instructions, participant handouts, or relevant job aids.

Blended Learning

A typical blended learning program is a series of self-paced assignments interspersed between live facilitator-led online events.

Integrating a Virtual Training Platform Into an LMS

One of the appeals of technology-based training is the ability to automate organizational learning. Automation means more efficiency because it frees up time for other tasks. An LMS allows an organization to easily track employee learning and provide an electronic repository for participant materials. Virtual training registrations can also be automated and predetermined communications sent to registered participants.

Therefore, when selecting a virtual training platform, it's important to understand its compatibility with the organization's LMS. And if it's compatible, determine the process to integrate the two platforms so they can be easily used in combination. According to Stacy Lindenberg, a noted LMS expert and principal at Talent Seed Consulting, these are the five most important considerations for organizations when integrating the two platforms:

- **Do your homework.** A virtual training platform's website may say it's compatible, but it's important to dig deeper into this generic statement. What does it mean to be compatible? Talk to others who use the two platforms (ask the supplier for references). Ask them, "What have you learned?" and "What would you do differently?" Look at industry reviews, such as Gartner's *Magic Quadrant* reports, to find out as much as you can in advance.
- **Don't make false assumptions about platform compatibility.** If the two platforms can "talk" to each other, what does that mean? Do they need a translator between them or can they work seamlessly together? You might find that it is better *not* to integrate them. A forced companionship might be more work than no communication at all.
- **Involve others in the organization.** It's a mistake to think that only the training department cares about the automated technology. Have an internal advisory council that represents all areas of the organization. These individuals can offer insights to systems, structures, and changes in their business units that would affect the systems. It's especially important to involve IT for their technology expertise and support.
- **Take advantage of all available features**. Stacy finds that many organizations are missing out on capabilities available to them in the combined platforms. It could be because the current administrator wasn't part of the original purchasing decision and isn't aware of the basic features. Or it could be that the platform has released updates with new functionality. Staying on top of the features can lead to greater efficiency and enhance compatibility.
- **Remember to measure impact.** Technology implementations require significant resources, and most organizations want to see a return on investment. Therefore, it's prudent to tie it back to cost savings or some other important organizational metric. For example, if participants now complete an online assignment or take assessments automatically as a result of the integration, this frees up significant time for people who used to have manual administrative tasks. Stacy says, "Look at where there are ways this can help different people in the organization and report on it."

Audio

Telephony is a broad term referring to the overall audio connection and telephone equipment used for the verbal portion of a virtual training session. The audio connection allows for verbal communication—a key component of engaging virtual training. Through telephony, a learner can hear the facilitator and talk with fellow class participants.

There are two types of audio connections that can be used for virtual training sessions: conference call (either stand-alone or integrated with the virtual platform) and VoIP.

If you choose a technology solution that uses conference calling, then each participant will need a reliable telephone connection and a headset for hands-free use. If you use VoIP, then each participant's computer will need to have a sound card, with either speakers and a microphone or a headset that combines the two.

Which audio connection type should you choose? It depends on the virtual platform software you'll use, the Internet bandwidth speeds available to participants, and your budget.

With conference calling, you have an extremely reliable audio connection through the telephone. The sound quality should be crystal-clear for everyone. In a stand-alone conference call, the audio is not connected to the virtual classroom software; they are independent of each other. While this setup provides redundancy in case of technical failure, it creates challenges for using breakout room features and other audio commands that are built into the software.

Integrated conference calling means that the audio and visual components of the virtual class are connected behind the scenes. Participants still use their telephone to dial into the audio portion of the call, but the audio commands, such as mute and unmute, can be controlled from the classroom's web platform. Features that use audio, such as breakout rooms, are available to all. It's also easy to tell who is speaking at any given moment, provided the software includes this feature.

VoIP audio is most commonly used for webcasts and webinars, in which the presenter is doing most of the talking. It's certainly possible to use VoIP connections for a virtual training class, if every participant has the appropriate hardware needed: a sound card, speakers, and a microphone. These pieces can be separate or combined as a mono or stereo headset that connects to the computer. When using VoIP, participants should be able to speak freely and easily during class, without having to "request microphone rights" to talk one at a time.

One advantage of VoIP is there is typically no additional cost associated with the audio. Since the audio travels through the software using the same connection, there is no extra cost tacked on. Consider it bundled audio with the software. Unfortunately, this is also the drawback of VoIP, because it takes extra Internet bandwidth space. In some cases, this extra space is enough to cause considerable quality issues and unclear sound connections.

As with everything regarding hardware, software, and telephony, you should spend considerable time testing prior to any virtual training session to discover any glitches well in advance and fix or work around them. When using VoIP, the visual and audio are using the same connection. Therefore, if the Internet connection is lost for any reason, all communication will be lost at the same time. So if the facilitator unexpectedly loses connectivity during class, he would not be able to continue until he re-establishes connection. If the facilitator had been using the telephone instead, then he could at least continue talking with participants and let them know what was happening while he reconnected.

When considering your audio choice, be sure to factor telephony costs into your budget, especially if you will have long-distance and international callers. Standard conference calling rates typically apply. For a summary of the features and pros and cons of each audio type, see Tool 2-8.

Internet Bandwidth

The single biggest technology challenge to successful virtual training isn't the software. It isn't the hardware. It isn't mobile devices. It isn't even a platform issue. It boils down to one thing—lack of sufficient Internet bandwidth.

The hardware, audio, and software come together over the Internet to create a virtual training class. Therefore, Internet connectivity should also be factored into the technology equation. Without a stable, reliable connection with suitable bandwidth for your needs, virtual training will not be successful. The Internet bandwidth available for each participant should be broad enough to support the class activities. There is nothing worse than a participant who continuously gets disconnected from a class because her Internet connection is not strong enough. The participant gets frustrated and wastes time logging in again. The facilitator or producer may have to stop and work to get that person reconnected. Other participants may be negatively affected while they wait for class to get back on track.

A worse scenario may occur when a participant stays connected to the class, but due to limited bandwidth has trouble seeing the screen or watching a video playback. That experience, from the participant point of view, is extremely frustrating. It's like knowing that everyone else is eating a tasty meal while you're getting only crumbs.

Some software platforms have built-in bandwidth buffers and play the audio at the same download rate as the participant bandwidth (Figure 2-3). Other platforms allow the host to change meeting room connectivity speeds to match the anticipated Internet bandwidth.

Bandwidth typically becomes an issue when participants log in from a spotty, publicly shared Wi-Fi connection. The best remedy for this issue is to instruct participants ahead of time on best practices for connecting to a virtual class. However, Internet bandwidth may also be an issue at a corporate location when the following factors are true:

- Multiple participants connect at the same time from the same location.
- A virtual class makes heavy use of multimedia, such as sharing video.
- Other business functions tie up bandwidth during certain timeframes.

To mitigate any Internet bandwidth issues that may occur and disrupt virtual training, thoroughly test for Internet connectivity issues by replicating the exact conditions under which it will be needed—at the same time of day, with a similar number of users, and so on. Make use of any features found in the virtual software platform that help control bandwidth. In addition, you might need to increase the amount of bandwidth available to your office locations by investing in an upgraded pipeline.

Figure 2-3. Adobe Connect Preferences: Screen Share

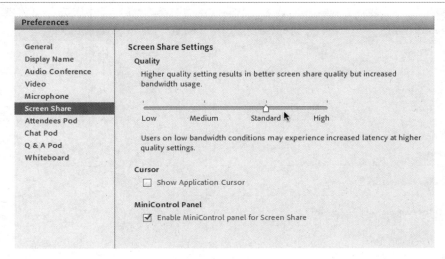

In Action: Selecting Technology at HDR

When HDR created a virtual training room—a dedicated space that facilitators could use for virtual training delivery—they outfitted it with the latest technology available. They included a computer, feedback TV monitors for the facilitator, conference call technology built into the room, webcams, microphones, and a document camera. They wanted to ensure that their facilitators had everything they could possibly need for a successful virtual training event.

Michael Merritt, HDR's e-learning development manager, says, "At the beginning, we didn't realize all the questions we needed to ask when setting up the room. We did a great job with most of it, but afterward, discovered several small details that became big issues. For example, our designers suggested a felt-type wall covering, which soundproofed the back and side wall to minimize noise from the larger auditorium next door. However, the felt's surface detail interfered with the camera's lenses, so we had to make some adjustments and paint the wall as we did with the others. We also realized that some of our equipment didn't have compatible inputs and therefore did not easily work together, and that's what you want when a facilitator walks in the room."

The good news is that HDR is preparing to open a new headquarters soon, and the virtual training room will move there. That means Michael and the team have used this room as a test for the next one. They will use the lessons they learned for even more success.

Tips, Tools, and Templates

To help you select technology for virtual training, here are some checklists, tools, and templates that will help you make the right choices for your organization.

Tool 2-1. Technology Planning Worksheet

Use the following worksheet to survey the technology that already exists in your organization. You may be surprised to discover some useful resources. You can also use this big-picture planning tool to determine which things you need to research and procure.

Technology Item	Have	Need	Comment
Hardware			
Laptops or computers for facilitators			
Laptops or computers for participants			
Headsets for facilitators			
Headsets for participants			
Webcams for facilitators			
Webcams for participants			
Software			
Virtual platform			
Learning management system			
Online portal for intersession collaboration			
Audio			
VoIP capability			
Integrated teleconference lines			
Internet Bandwidth (sufficient for virtual training)			
Other Needs Unique to Your Organization			

Tool 2-2. Building a Relationship With IT

Successful virtual training requires a close partnership between the training and IT departments. And close partnerships are created through communication and relationship building.

7 Tips for Partnering With IT

To partner with your IT department, consider the following ideas:

- **Find an executive champion.** Gain the support of a senior manager who believes in virtual training and the positive impact it can have on the organization. Ask this internal champion to consistently advocate for and support virtual training, and to help you secure resources. Also request their assistance in eliminating any red tape that might exist between the training and IT departments.

- **Discover common business goals and drivers.** Latch onto a corporate initiative that both groups have a stake in to find common ground. For example, are both departments trying to reduce printing costs, and therefore potentially interested in using the electronic file transfer features found in virtual classroom platforms?

- **Build a relationship.** Even in very large organizations that have separated silos, large departments are made up of individual people. Start getting to know the individuals within the IT department and building relationships. You might begin with a short meeting to find common interests, and stay in touch to compare notes.

- **Clearly explain what is needed for virtual training and why.** Most IT professionals pride themselves on meeting customer needs and helping the organization be successful. Therefore, if they clearly understand what and why a requirement is needed, they may be open to making it happen.

- **Build a business case.** Use Tool 1-11 from chapter 1 to build a business case for your IT requests. Put yourself in their shoes and consider what benefits appeal to them. Select the best time and method to make your request.

- **Investigate shared costs and shared responsibility models.** Many IT departments are spread thin and resistant to new technology because they'd be unable to take on additional responsibilities. Or, they assume that the budget for virtual training will affect their department's bottom line. Therefore, do your homework on virtual training technology needs and explore shared solutions. Consider suppliers who provide externally hosted programs, or who can provide external support for deployment.

- **Communicate, communicate, communicate.** Ongoing communication is key in any relationship, including the partnership between the training and IT departments. Schedule regular check-in meetings to keep the lines of communication open. Frequently discuss items of interest to both groups, including changes in technology requirements and annual updates to departmental goals.

Questions to Answer From an IT Perspective

When you approach your IT department to seek approvals for purchasing a virtual training platform, it's essential to be prepared. IT will have a different perspective on considering software solutions. They may ask questions such as the ones in this list. Use the following worksheet to compile your responses:

1.   Will it work with our already existing systems? Is it compatible?

2.   Will we buy and install it, or will it be hosted by a supplier?

3.   If we buy it, who will install it? Maintain it? Support it?

4.   If it's hosted, how will the hosting company protect our data?

5.   What IT resources—initially and ongoing—will be needed to support the program?

When you partner with IT to make your technology selections—hardware and software—you will end up with a choice that appeals to both sides. You will also have a working partnership that will strengthen your virtual training implementation.

Tool 2-3. Common Virtual Classroom Platform Tools

Most virtual classroom software programs have similar features and functionality. When assessing your needs, use this table to compare platform benefits. Note that this is not an exhaustive list of all tools found in every platform.

Tool	Description	Sample Use
Document sharing	A commonly used feature that allows the facilitator to share documents (such as slides) for participants to see	Display content and group activity instructions onscreen.
Chat	Enables communication between and among participants through typed messages	Encourage dialogue and discussion during a program.
Annotate and draw	Allows for real-time drawing and typing on top of shared documents or a whiteboard	Highlight key words or graphics onscreen to maintain visual interest. Also allow participants to draw or type onscreen and on documents during group activities.
Whiteboard	A blank screen that can be drawn or typed on. Similar to classroom chart paper, but in electronic form	Group brainstorming activities when allowing participants to use the annotation tools.
Status indicators	Lets participants click on a button to display their real-time status	Ask yes/no or agree/disagree questions that generate discussion.
Raise hand	Gives participants the opportunity to raise their hand virtually	Ask individuals to voluntarily respond by raising their hand.
Poll	Asks multiple-choice or short-answer questions	Ask challenging questions to quiz participants' knowledge of a topic.
Breakouts	Allows participants to divide into smaller groups	Complete role plays to practice skills.
File and material distribution	Offers handouts and other paper-based resources through electronic file transfer	Distribute participant materials during an event.
Tests and quizzes	Creates test questions on the training topic	Check for knowledge transfer and comprehension.
Application and screen sharing	Displays an application on the facilitators' screen so that all participants can see it	Conduct a software demonstration.

Tool 2-4. Comparison Between Platform Tools for Meetings, Training, and Webcasts

Many virtual platforms have different product versions available: one product for large webcasts, and another product for small group training programs. The versions have different functionality based on the purpose of the online event. For example, a webcast product may keep the participant list visible only to presenters, while the training version shows it to all. Or a webinar product may have chat and poll features, and the training version adds in breakout functionality. See the following chart for a list of typical differences between platform products.

Tool	Meeting	Training	Webcast
Chat	Both public and private chat available	Both public and private chat available	Public chat typically not available; participants may be able to send a private message to hosts and presenters
Annotate and draw	Typically available	Typically available	Usually only available to hosts and presenters
Whiteboard	Typically available	Typically available	May not be available
Status indicators	Nonexistent	Typically available	If available, individual results usually only visible to hosts and presenters
Raise hand	Individual results usually only visible to hosts and presenters	Results visible to all	Individual results usually only visible to hosts and presenters
Poll	Typically available	Typically available	Typically available
Breakouts	Nonexistent	Typically available	Nonexistent
File and material distribution	Typically available	Typically available	May not be available
Application sharing	Typically available	Typically available	May not be available
Tests and quizzes	Nonexistent	Typically available	Nonexistent

Tool 2-5. Questions to Ask During a Virtual Training Platform Demo

When you are selecting a virtual classroom platform, it's helpful to see it in action before making a purchase. If you're able to view a demonstration of the platform, here are some questions to ask:

1. Which product or version of the platform is being demonstrated?

2. What other products or versions of the platform exist?

3. What's unique about this platform?

4. What specific tools and features are available in this platform? Will you demonstrate each one?

5. How many hosts or presenters can be in a session at the same time?

6. How many participants can be in a session at the same time?

7. What tools or features are only available to hosts or presenters?

8. What privileges can be granted to participants?

9. How many simultaneous breakout rooms can an event have?

10. How are virtual events created? What information is needed to create an event? Is there a calendar plug-in for invitations?

11. How does the platform handle Internet bandwidth and connectivity issues?

12. What audio options are available with this platform? If integrated conference calling is available, what are its features and limitations? For example, are international numbers available in the countries where we have office locations?

13. How does the license model work for this platform?

14. Is this platform compatible with our learning management system?

Tool 2-6. Comparing Hosted Versus On-Site Technology Solutions

Some virtual classroom platforms offer the ability to host internally. Internal hosting is sometimes referred to as "on-premise hosting," while external hosting can be called a "software-as-a-service" model. When would an internal hosting choice be right for your organization? Consider these advantages and disadvantages.

Advantages and Disadvantages of Internal Hosting:

- ☐ Organization has control over installation and maintenance

- ☐ Data are backed up along with the rest of the organization's data

- ☐ Available for Internal access without firewall issues

- ☐ May need to purchase additional internal server space

- ☐ Need assigned IT support to maintain programs

Advantages and Disadvantages of Supplier or External Hosting:

- ☐ Less burden on internal IT resources

- ☐ Ease of installation and use—often immediate

- ☐ Automatic software updates when new versions are released

- ☐ Usually less initial setup costs

- ☐ Support often included with hosted license

- ☐ May have firewall issues when accessing an external site

- ☐ May not have control over data backup frequency

- ☐ May have ongoing monthly or annual hosting fees

Tool 2-7. Checklist for Selecting a Platform

When selecting a virtual platform, start with a list of features you need. Do you need breakout groups so that you can have small group activities? Do you need video streaming for demonstrations? Do you need a private chat option for the type of communication you plan to use? Do you need compatibility with a specific LMS? All these will help you narrow down which supplier's virtual training platform will be the best fit for your organization. Use the following form to help you keep track of your choices:

Features	Supplier 1	Supplier 2	Supplier 3	Supplier 4
Platform Features				
Shared document file type requirements	☐	☐	☐	☐
Media file playback (audio and video)	☐	☐	☐	☐
Chat	☐	☐	☐	☐
Annotation or drawing privileges	☐	☐	☐	☐
Whiteboard features	☐	☐	☐	☐
Raise hand and/or status indicators	☐	☐	☐	☐
Breakout groups	☐	☐	☐	☐
Other	☐	☐	☐	☐
Audio Features				
Integrated conference calling available?	☐	☐	☐	☐
VoIP available?	☐	☐	☐	☐
Features	**Supplier 1**	**Supplier 2**	**Supplier 3**	**Supplier 4**
Other Features				
Compatible with mobile device (for participants)?	☐	☐	☐	☐
Able to have multiple hosts and facilitators?	☐	☐	☐	☐
Compatible with your organization's LMS?	☐	☐	☐	☐
Internet bandwidth issues?	☐	☐	☐	☐
Other Considerations Unique to Your Organization				
	☐	☐	☐	☐
	☐	☐	☐	☐
	☐	☐	☐	☐

Tool 2-8. Audio Options Worksheet

As you decide what type of audio to use for your virtual training platform, consider what's best for your organization. Use the following pros and cons (benefits and drawbacks) list to help you determine the best solution.

Audio Type	Pros	Cons
VoIP	· Included with the virtual training platform · Host has full control over audio commands (i.e., mute user, mute all) · No obvious cost to users · Easy to use with very little setup required to connect	· Uses Internet bandwidth, which may be limited and therefore have intermittent or frequent poor audio quality
Integrated	· Possibly included with the virtual training platform, if purchased with the license · Typically a high-quality audio experience · Host has full control over audio commands (i.e., mute user, mute all) · Allows for full use of the platform features that rely on audio	· Teleconference charges billed per user, per minute
Separate	· Participants may already be familiar with conference numbers and commands (if using the company conference line)	· Host has no control over audio commands (i.e., mute user, mute all) · Platform features that use audio—such as speaker identification and breakouts—will be limited or unavailable

Which one will be best for your organization's virtual training?

❏ VoIP

❏ Integrated

❏ Separate conference line

❏ Combination of the above. Explain:

Tool 2-9. Sample RFP Template

If your organization requires a formal request for proposal (RFP) to consider new technology, ask these questions and seek out this information about possible virtual training platforms.

1. Please provide general information about your company. Where are your headquarters? How long have you been in business?

2. How long has this product been on the market? What is the current version?

3. What are the features of the specific product? How do these features support interactive virtual training?

4. What are the technical requirements to use the platform, such as hardware or browsers?

5. What makes your product unique? Why should we select it?

6. Are there installation or implementation services offered as part of the purchase price?

7. What training do you provide at initial purchase or installation? What ongoing support is available?

8. How often is the product upgraded? What is the cost of an upgrade?

9. What hosting options are available? If your product is hosted on your internal servers, what are your backup and data recovery policies?

10. What is the pricing structure (per user, per installation, per developer)?

11. Are teleconferencing lines included with the product? If so, what is the per-minute cost?

12. Please provide at least three client references of current clients who are actively using your product.

13. Why should we select your product for our organization's virtual training programs?

Tool 2-10. Technology Requirements for Facilitators and Producers Checklist

If you're considering only the technology needed for facilitators and producers of a virtual training program, use this checklist.

Hardware

❐ Computer or laptop (mobile device not recommended)

❐ Second computer or laptop (mobile device not recommended)

Software

❐ Required downloads or plug-ins for virtual platform

Telephony

❐ Hands-free headset*

❐ Reliable telephone connection or VoIP*

Internet Connection

❐ Speed test for appropriate bandwidth*

---

*Note that facilitators and producers may also need to plan for redundancies in telephony and possibly Internet connection, in case of unexpected technical issues. For example, if the facilitator works from a home office, she should have a backup telephone (such as a mobile device) and an alternative Internet connection (such as an air card or nearby Wi-Fi hotspot).

Tool 2-11. Technology Requirements for Participants Checklist

If you're considering just the technology needed for participants in a virtual training program, use this checklist.

Hardware

❐ Computer, laptop, or mobile device (compatible with platform)

❐ Sound card for audio or video playback (if needed)

Software

❐ Required downloads or plug-ins

Telephony

❐ Hands-free headset

❐ Reliable telephone connection or VoIP

Internet Connection

❐ Speed test for appropriate bandwidth

CHAPTER 3

Design Content

Good design is a critical success factor for effective virtual training. Good design engages participants and leads to learning outcomes—two key components to effective learning transfer. The design should be well planned and thought out so that your training goals are met.

Good design is more than just creating slides. It's more than just scheduling speakers for an online panel discussion and hoping that learning will take place. It's more than just taking a traditional in-person class and transferring it word-for-word to an online one. Instead, good design is about creating a high-quality learning experience. And going one step further—a *great* design allows learning to take place and skills to be transferred back to the workplace.

How do you create great virtual training designs? It begins with skilled instructional designers who are comfortable with technology, can convert programs into a new format, and are able to capture learner attention with interactive elements. You may already have designers who can do these things, but if not, then you'll want to enhance their skills to include virtual training.

This chapter will help you both upskill your instructional designers and create great virtual training designs. It provides tools, templates, tips, and resources to guide you from start to finish. Whether you are designing a one-way presentation, a panel discussion, a facilitated meeting, or an interactive virtual training class, you can use the tools in this chapter to plan your online event. These tools encourage a planned-out process and dialogue between hosts, presenters, facilitators, and the audience.

The Initial Step

When you begin to design a course, it's tempting to open a new blank slide presentation and start writing, or take a slide presentation you've used in an in-person class and believe you already have a design. But imagine if you were to build a house by starting to dig the foundation before creating a blueprint, or by using a blueprint that doesn't fit the terrain of the land. Neither method brings success. Starting to create slides (or repurpose existing ones) before you have a learning blueprint prepared will not lead to success either.

As discussed in chapter 1, one of the first steps of any virtual training project is to define it. That definition will drive your design. Determine your overarching goal for the session. What are you trying to accomplish? What topic are you trying to convey? What information should be shared, or what skill needs to be learned? The answers to these questions will influence the program design.

Other considerations include your participants: How many will you invite to each session? What do they already know about the topic? What experience do they have that you can draw upon? What questions are they likely to ask? What concerns will they share?

Given the answers to these questions, what's the best way to achieve your goals? Do you need a main presenter who will provide one-way communication to a large audience? Will it be a facilitated meeting with every participant taking an active role in the speaking? Will it be a panel discussion with interactive questions and answers from a large audience? Will it be a small-group training class that requires participants to have hands-on skill practice?

Each of these examples represents a different type of session, and therefore will have a different type of design. Once you determine your goal and the type of session you will have, you can design appropriately.

It's a common mistake to mix the session types in thought and design. In other words, you might think you are designing a training class when it's actually a simple presentation with one-way communication. Avoid this error by designing a session that builds on your established framework and desired outcomes.

When clients ask for help in designing a virtual training program, my first response is to start asking questions. I ask them to tell me more about the program; what are its goals? If they describe a presentation or SME panel discussion, then the design would be different than if they described a specific skill that learners needed to try out and practice through role plays. Both types of programs could fit well in a virtual program, but the program designs would be quite different. For the presentation, I'd design an interactive lecture for a large audience, say 75 people, with many polls, chat questions, and captivating visuals on the slides. And for the skill-building program with role plays, I'd keep it to a small audience—fewer than 20—and include intensive discussions, breakouts, and small group case studies.

A 3-Step Process

This is the three-step design process I follow and have found to be successful. It was introduced in detail in *The Virtual Training Guidebook*. A summary is provided here for reference:

1. Select the best format for each learning objective.
2. Shape appropriate learning activities.
3. Structure a logical flow.

In step 1, you are determining what content belongs in the virtual training class and what topics are conducive to pre-work or other offline activities that occur outside the virtual class-room. You are also ensuring that your program has learning objectives that have been reviewed for validity. When you examine the objectives to determine the best format, you are creating the structure of your virtual training program. Most often, your design will become a series of virtual sessions, or a blended learning program with a mixture of delivery methods combined to create a curriculum.

When choosing the best format, it's important to consider the type of learning objective (knowledge, skill, attitude), along with the topic at hand. Knowledge topics can often be learned in a self-paced format, such as reading a book or reviewing an infographic. But some sensitive topics, such as dealing with change or having difficult conversations, might be best delivered with an experienced trainer guiding the discussion. Note that your design may very well take the shape of a blended learning program: a series of self-paced assignments interspersed between live facilitator-led online events.

In addition, consider the participants and their comfort level with technology, their physical locations, and anything else you know about them that could influence the way they learn best. All these items should factor into your decision about the best format, and therefore will influence the overall design.

In step 2, you are choosing the methods by which the learning will take place. In other words, you draw up the blueprint for each virtual training class. What activities will be done, with which platform features? Will you use the chat window for a discussion topic? Will you ask participants to brainstorm using their drawing tools on a whiteboard? Will you set up breakout groups that participants can use to role-play and receive feedback? In this step, you also choose what activities could take place outside the live event, such as asking learners to complete a short reading assignment before or after.

Finally, in step 3, you'll place the activities into a logical order and sequence the virtual training program so that it flows well. In this step, you'll pay special attention to the program opening as well as the arrangement of each activity. Both areas are of special importance because they provide an opportunity to capture and maintain participant involvement in their own learning. If you have multiple virtual events taking place in a series, you'll also sequence the order of each one. Refer to Tool 3-1 to use the three-step process when you design your own virtual training programs.

Tips, Tools, and Templates

Now that we've set the stage with the process, let's turn to the tools that can help you make a great design happen. Note that the tools in this chapter focus more on the overall design of your program (step 1), while the next chapter will dive deeper into developing activities within your program (step 2).

Tool 3-1. Template for the 3-Step Design Process

This checklist will walk you through the three-step process. Begin by listing all learning objectives in the first column. Then, consider each objective as you work your way across each row. When finished filling in the table, review the structure and flow. This will become the basis of your design document.

1. Select the best format for each learning objective.
2. Shape appropriate learning activities.
3. Structure a logical flow.

Training Program Name:

Learning Objective	Factors That Determine the Best Way to Learn	Other Influencing Factors	Activity Options	Comments
Example: "Select the correct online form for each type of customer request."	Skill-based objective, want the learners to practice choosing the correct form.	Most learners will already know where to find the online forms; they just need criteria to select the right one.	Present onscreen scenario and poll to select correct form; use breakout groups to complete case studies.	Need to ensure that all learners get the opportunity to practice this skill.

Tool 3-2. Best Practices for Converting In-Person Classes to Online Classes

For many organizations, the best way to start with a virtual training initiative is to take an in-person classroom program and move it online. The learning objectives have been created, the program content exists, and the participant activities have already been designed.

You might think, "These items just need to be transferred to the virtual classroom," which sounds simple. However, there's more to it than just using the same slides and activities. Those items need to be adapted to the web classroom platform. It's not a one-to-one transfer; it's a one-to-many transformation—the timing needs to be reworked, the materials need to be reformatted, and the activities need to be realigned. Here are five guidelines for converting in-person classes to online ones:

1. **Maintain the program interactivity.** If it's interactive in person, keep it interactive online. Don't fall into the trap of taking a highly interactive classroom program and turning it into an online lecture. Use the platform tools to maintain the interaction. Find ways to emulate the activities and require participant engagement.

2. **Look for ways to involve every participant in every activity.** In the classroom, a discussion might mean one person speaking at a time. But in the online classroom, a multithreaded conversation can happen in the chat window. Everyone can respond to poll questions. Drawing tools can be used on whiteboards. Make liberal use of these online classroom features to invite everyone into the conversation.

3. **Keep the participant counts the same.** If the program is designed for 20 people in the traditional classroom, then there should be a maximum of 20 people in the online classroom. Just because you can fit more people in an online room doesn't mean you should. In fact, it may be even better to have fewer participants in your online event so that you can maximize discussion and dialogue opportunities with a smaller group.

4. **Create smaller chunks of learning**. Most virtual training programs are no more than 60-90 minutes in length. If your classroom program is longer than this, consider breaking it down into short segments placed in a series. It would be better to have five one-hour virtual events than one five-hour session.

5. **Determine what needs to be done in the online classroom versus what can be a self-paced assignment.** Not everything in the in-person class needs to take place in the online classroom. Is there a video that participants can watch on their own time? Are there assessments they could take after the class and then share with their managers for accountability? Think creatively about the online program structure.

A Sample Conversion Outline

A client wanted to convert a three-and-a-half-hour in-person leadership program to the virtual classroom. After reviewing the program learning objectives, activity outlines, and the organization's design principles, I created a detailed design document to explain how the activities could be replicated online (and which ones would not). Here is an excerpt of this document (Figure 3-1).

Figure 3-1. Design Document for Conversion Outline

Time in Minutes	Objective	Topic	Activity or Learning Method
	Start-Before-the-Start/Soft Opening	• Make "soft" introductions • Get acquainted with web platform features (if needed) • Respond to opening question	• Invite learners to introduce themselves verbally and in chat (chat) • Ask learners to respond to onscreen poll: "What's your experience leading virtual teams? Leading one now? Will lead one in the future? Have lead in past? None of the above?" (poll) • Display housekeeping and ground rules (share document or in notes) • Music playing in background for sound check • Handout available if needed (file share)
6	Opening	• Welcome/Set Stage	• Facilitator welcome and define virtual team • Ask learners to respond to poll: "Which leadership responsibilities are unique to leading virtual teams?" (add more in chat) (poll and chat) • Reference learner responses to poll question (allows learners who did not respond earlier a chance to respond) • Debrief with overview of virtual leadership (slides) • Reference learner introductions already in chat, and ask learners to expand in chat about their virtual team
8	Recognize factors that affect virtual team performance	• Video: A Team in Crisis	• Learners asked to brainstorm characteristics of team at maximum performance (whiteboard or chat) • Facilitator sets up video purpose (include tech tips) • "What to watch for" questions placed in notes or chat • Show video (invite note taking and responding in chat while video plays) • Learners "raise hand" at end of video • Video debrief discussion (verbal or in chat)

In Action: Converting an In-Person Class to a Virtual Experience

In response to a business need, Coventry Health Care's learning and performance department converted an in-person classroom program to an online virtual one. The request came from the operations group, which needed to cross-train a group of new hires who were geographically dispersed and working from home. An eight-hour in-person new hire program already existed, but this opportunity called for a virtual solution.

"We knew that this new hire virtual class could not be approached the same way, therefore we met with the stakeholder to conduct a thorough needs analysis," says senior learning consultant Mark Aronson. "We asked questions to determine their post-training expectations, and to clarify the knowledge, skills, and abilities needed afterward—immediately, 30 days, and 90 days. We also reviewed the old curriculum for its content."

Mark and his team approached the new virtual curriculum through the lens of "context vs. content." They mapped out ways to train the context of the new hires' work flow without overwhelming them with content. In other words, after laying the foundation and providing a big picture of how their role fits in with the structure, they introduced new content only when it applied to the next step of their work flow. This approach provided a logical structure and flow to the new virtual curriculum.

The team also recognized the challenges of virtual training—no visual cues, no human contact, and potential technology issues. So they designed the new virtual program with those factors in mind. For example, they asked the new hires to provide a photo and displayed them onscreen during introductions. They also gave participants the opportunity to speak for two to three minutes about themselves to mimic some of the natural conversation that would happen during an in-person class, and they used webcams periodically throughout the program. Finally, they used all the platform tools available—whiteboards, chat, polling, quizzes, emoticons, videos, screensharing, and hands-on practice—to make the program as interactive as possible.

The resulting virtual program was a four-week blended curriculum. They used an internal social media site to host discussion threads, short video clips (referred to as "learning soundbites"), links and materials needed for the program, and a blog for sharing information.

"Some participants were initially skeptical about four weeks of virtual learning, but many of those participants indicated afterward that they preferred virtual to classroom," says Aronson. "The experience prepared them to do their jobs within the framework of a virtual environment."

Tool 3-3. The ADDIE Model and This Book

There are many different instructional design models available for use. The ADDIE model, described here, remains one of the most common. *ADDIE* is an acronym for the steps of the model: analyze, design, develop, implement, and evaluate. It's a useful logistical framework for designing virtual training. In addition, the structure and flow of this book loosely follows the ADDIE model, as shown in the following table.

Phase	Description	Where to Find in This Book
Analyze	Sometimes called "training needs assessment," it includes: • definition of organizational and individual performance results • identifying performance measures for the competencies or tasks to be taught • identifying skill and knowledge requirements • determining level of instruction needed based on performer analysis • creating an evaluation strategy for training.	Chapter 1: Get Ready
Design	Creation of a training strategy that includes: • learning objectives for each competency or task • assessments or tests to show mastery • training prerequisites • sequence and structure of topics and lessons • selection of instructional delivery media and methods.	Chapter 3: Design Content
Develop	Production activity that includes creating: • participant learning materials (workbooks, handouts, practice instructions, case studies, etc.) • facilitator guide (where appropriate) • visual aids (slides, etc.) • test of materials (pilot test).	Chapter 4: Develop Activities
Implement	Putting the training program into action, including: • communicating with participants about the upcoming training program • conducting the training program.	Chapter 5: Work With Facilitators and Producers Chapter 6: Prepare Participants
Evaluate	Review and revision, including: • review and evaluation of each ADDIE phase to ensure it is accomplishing what it needs to • evaluation of the instructional effectiveness of the training program through assessments, observation of performance on the job, and measurement of organizational impact • revision of the training program.	Chapter 7: Evaluate Results

Source: ADDIE descriptions adapted from ATD's Designing Learning Certificate Program.

Tool 3-4. Sample Design Standards Checklist for Virtual Training

When you start using virtual training, create a set of design standards that everyone will follow. These standards will become the basis for all design decisions; they're like branding guidelines made by an organization's marketing department. Here's a sample design standards checklist.

General Design

- ❏ Virtual training classes shouldn't be more than 90 minutes, and ideally no longer than 60.
- ❏ If the program content spans more than one virtual event (for example, 120 minutes total for a series of three virtual events), each event should have short, self-directed participant assignments in between each one.
- ❏ The design should be "platform neutral," and easily adapted to major virtual classroom software platforms. Notes should be included in the facilitator guide. along with directions to adjust the program, depending on the features of the virtual classroom platform.

Activity Standards

- ❏ The design should be interactive, with participant engagement every three to five minutes.
- ❏ Include a facilitator guide with acvtivity instructions. Base activities on the learning objectives.
- ❏ Facilitator guides should include introductory notes for the trainer or producer to check virtual classroom settings (such as participant privileges and rights). This information should be included in a "trainer and producer setup" section.
- ❏ All guides should include instructions for at least one onscreen activity for participants who join early. The design should also include the screen changing at least every minute. This could be through slide animation and builds, moving to the next slide, annotation on the slide, or moving to another activity.
- ❏ The design should make use of all common virtual classroom platform tools, such as chat, whiteboard, annotation, polling, and breakouts.

Visual Aids and Slides

- ❏ Slides should include lean text and use graphics as much as possible.
- ❏ Bulleted lists slides should be used sparingly. If used, they should have no more than three to four bullet points.
- ❏ Slides should have a white or light background and use common sans serif fonts.
- ❏ Slides should use builds to help keep the screen changing frequently.
- ❏ Activity directions should be posted onscreen as well as in the participant handout.

Participant Materials

- ❏ Participants will receive a checklist with instructions on what to do in preparation for the program.
- ❏ Every program should include at least one participant workbook or job aid. This document should contain reference material that can be used back on the job, and should not include copies of the slides or other facilitator-only materials.
- ❏ Handouts should be no more than 15 pages in length, with consideration for no wasted paper. For example, do not have a blank section break page.
- ❏ Handouts should include activity instructions for any complex virtual class activities.

Tool 3-5. Checklist for Upskilling Traditional Instructional Designers in Virtual Training

An instructional designer who begins to create virtual training programs will find that there are many similarities between designing traditional classroom programs and online ones. However, there are also enough differences—both subtle and not-so-subtle–that additional skills are needed. For example, virtual training designers need to know how to design learning activities for remotely connected facilitators and participants, and how to design activities that make use of the online platform tools. They also need to provide detailed technical instructions for facilitators and producers to follow.

Upskilling Traditional Instructional Designers in Virtual Training

If you're in charge of upskilling instructional designers for the virtual classroom—or if you are a designer yourself—here are some tips to follow:

- **Brush-up on basic instructional design skills.** These skills are the foundational starting point for any design project.

- **Commit** to following your organization's virtual training design standards and processes. If you do not have a set of standards, see Tool 3-4 for a sample.

- **Learn every tool and feature of your virtual classroom platform.** You have to know which platform features exist and how they work to design activities that use them.

- **Remember what you know about adult learners.** Just because the delivery format is different doesn't mean adult learning basics has changed. Apply what you know to be true about adult learners. They want learning to be involved, engaged, and interactive.

- **Make extra effort to design for participant engagement and interactivity.** Get participants talking and interacting with one another early in the design. A successful virtual class design includes not only facilitator-participant interaction, but also collaboration between learners.

- **Include technical instructions for setup and delivery of every class activity.** Facilitators and producers will rely on your specific directions for using the platform tools to enable learning.

Tool 3-6. Virtual Instructional Designer Job Description

If you are hiring a new instructional designer to join your training team, or retooling your existing instructional designer job descriptions to include virtual training skills, consider the following sample job description as a starting point:

- Designs and develops virtual training instructional materials using the ADDIE methodology.
- Collaborates with SMEs and stakeholders to gather content information and requirements, define learning objectives, and determine program formats.
- Identifies measurable learning objectives and business outcomes for each virtual training program.
- Uses a variety of techniques to define, structure, and sequence instructional content and strategies.
- Creates and maintains project plans for each design project.
- Designs and develops participant and facilitator guides, slides and other visual aids, and other learning materials required for virtual training.
- Builds on-the-job application tools and learning aids into the design.
- Applies adult learning theory to all virtual training designs.
- Builds relationships among stakeholders, including subject matter experts, at each step of the design process.
- Conducts material reviews with appropriate parties, such as subject matter experts, other members of the design team, and learners.
- Facilitates virtual walk-throughs of program content to ensure smooth hand-offs to the delivery team.
- Stays current in virtual learning design trends and platform updates to continually recommend innovative learning solutions.

Tool 3-7. Components to Design and Develop for a Virtual Training Initiative

When planning a virtual training design project, it's helpful to have a checklist of typically created items. Use this material list as a guideline.

Materials		Description
❐	**Graphic or media elements**	• Review your design document and make a list of major graphics or media (such as prerecorded videos) that will need to be produced for the program. • Meet with graphic designers or media resources to discuss design and production of these course elements. • Consider the platform technology capabilities. For example, is there enough bandwidth to play videos, or should a series of screenshot captures be used instead?
❐	**Facilitator and producer guide**	• Write a facilitator and producer guide to include virtual platform setup requirements, required participant permissions, expected activity timings, discussion questions, and any other necessary information to effectively deliver the program.
❐	**Participant materials**	• Create participant materials to include reference information and on-the-job task instructions. • Incorporate needed examples, activity instructions, and practice exercises. • If participants are expected to print their own materials, keep pages to a minimum required number.
❐	**Visual aids**	• Identify content to be included in slides. • Identify other needed visual content, such as stock photos for slides.
❐	**Support materials**	• Create participant job aids and other reference information. • Identify other needed virtual classroom content, such as whiteboards, polls, or activity requirements.

Tool 3-8. 5 Tips for Partnering With SMEs on Virtual Class Design

Virtual training designs are rarely produced in isolation. Because a designer is often not an expert on the training topic, a key relationship is the one between designer and subject matter expert. In my experience, SMEs are extremely knowledgeable and want to include everything there is to know, instead of only what's important to know. They also don't have much time to help with the design. Therefore, use these tips to establish a quality partnership between designers and SMEs.

1. **Start off on the right foot.** In your initial communication, discuss project goals and how you each view the project. Create an atmosphere of respect and trust. Talk about expected time commitments so that there are no surprises later. The SME has another full-time job (and your plate is probably full as well), so commit to respecting each other's time.

2. **Establish a positive working relationship.** Discuss roles and responsibilities, along with milestones for completion. View the relationship as a partnership; each of you has an important part. Involve the SME in the project from the beginning and value their assistance. Thank them for contributing to the success of the project.

3. **Make their job easy.** While the SME is the expert, things will go more smoothly if you learn as much as you can about the topic. Familiarize yourself with the topic's terminology so that you can have productive conversations. Show the SME examples of virtual training projects you've created so they are familiar with the type of information you need.

4. **Ask questions.** A SME may already have formal presentations or information guides on the topic, but they might not be ideal to use in a training program. Review the information, but ask follow-up questions about how learners use the content, common challenges, and why things are done in a certain way. Also ask about frequent questions for helpful tips and "hacks" to share.

5. **Communicate, communicate, communicate.** As mentioned in Tool 2-2, communication is of critical importance. Keep the lines of communication open with the SME as you create the virtual training program. Avoid making assumptions, but instead clarify and confirm as needed. Provide feedback and be open to feedback.

Tool 3-9. Guidelines for Shaping a Blended Learning Curriculum

Virtual learning events often take place in the context of a larger blended learning curriculum. Therefore, it's common to design virtual training in conjunction with an overall learning solution. For example, your management development program might work best as a blended program that has four live online events interspersed with three self-paced assignments. Or it could be a mix of in-person classes and live online events. The point is that there's no single right way to organize blended programs. Instead there are some general guidelines to follow.

When determining if a blended learning solution is the right answer, you can look to the four main questions I posed in *The Virtual Training Guidebook*. (I refer to them as "the 4 Ts.") Consider the topic and its learning objectives, and ask the following questions:

> ## Using an LMS With a Blended Learning Curriculum
>
> Blended learning programs typically combine multiple learning assets in a variety of formats into one cohesive curriculum. Organizations can use a learning management system to store these items and link them together. The LMS provides a central repository that makes it easy for learners to access program components, and easy for administrators to track learner progress through a course.

1. What **type** of learning objectives are they? Are they knowledge, skill, or attitude? Knowledge objectives can often be learned in a passive way, like reading a description or watching a demonstration, while skill objectives need to be learned by doing the skill. And attitude objectives usually need to be learned through social methods, such as talking with a trusted, experienced mentor or experiencing peer pressure in a social setting. Therefore, you could take some (or all) of the knowledge objective topics and assign them as reading assignments for learners to complete on their own time. You could take the skill topics and build in hands-on labs, or breakout group role plays. Or, if the skill needs to be done in the workplace, you could design a practice assignment for learners to complete in between live events and report on progress.

2. Is **togetherness** required? Do participants need to be together to learn the topic? If they do, then including it in a live online session makes sense. For example, if participants are learning how to hold performance review conversations with underperforming employees and they need to practice replying to defensive responses, then the best design format would include role-play practices with guided feedback from an expert facilitator.

3. What **technology** capabilities are available? Hopefully you have selected a robust virtual classroom platform that includes all the features you need for online learning. However, the question of technology should be factored into your design decisions. For example, you might wish to conduct video role plays by asking

participants to turn on their webcams and have conversations with one another to practice a skill. But the Internet bandwidth and slower-than-ideal connection speeds might prevent this choice from being an option. Technology shouldn't be your sole deciding factor for a learning design, but it will play a role in the decision.

4. What **trainee** information (demographics, background) should be considered? You may think based on the previous questions that the curriculum belongs entirely online in a self-paced format, but the reality of your learner situations means that in-person events are the only way they will learn the content. The participants might not be motivated to complete assignments on their own, or they might not have the technology or time available to learn that way. Or you may realize that the participants have strong feelings about the topic (for instance, if the training topic introduces a brand-new process change that will conjure up strongly held opinions), and therefore want to ensure that a skilled facilitator is available to lead everyone through the issues.

Use the following table to record your notes about the four Ts as they relate to your own training curriculum.

Guideline	Notes
Types of learning objectives	
Togetherness required?	
Technology capabilities	
Trainee backgrounds	

The Importance of Learning Objectives

Learning objectives are short, specific statements of what a person needs to be able to do at the end of a learning event. Objectives should be measurable and observable, and are tied to what a person needs to know or do on the job.

According to Julie Dirksen (2012), in her book *Design for How People Learn,* well-written learning objectives should indicate "something the learner would actually do in the real world" and something you can "tell when they've done it."

Even if you have a situation in which knowledge is the outcome, there is usually some way that learners need to act upon that knowledge. Therefore, actions in your learning objectives should be an active verb. One sign of a weak learning objective is the use of *know* or *understand* as the verb, because neither of those actions can be measured.

To illustrate, consider the difference between these examples:

"At the end of this training session, a participant will know three techniques for responding to an upset customer."

Or

"At the end of this training session, a participant will be able to:

- Recognize three techniques for responding to upset customers.
- Select an appropriate technique based upon an upset customer's situation.
- Use the appropriate technique to respond to an upset customer."

Notice how the second example is much richer, ties to what the learner would need to do on the job, and enables you to plan in more detail what the training program needs to cover.

Tool 3-10. Sample Template for Blended Learning Design

When designing a blended curriculum, I like to sketch out the design in a visual format. At first, I'll use sticky notes on a whiteboard, and then migrate to a digital format. Figure 3-2 is an example of a four-month management development program that includes a blend of traditional classroom programs, self-paced e-learning assignments, live online virtual classes, and individual coaching for each participant. The four Ts were used as guidelines to determine which topics belonged in the classroom and which ones would work well as individual assignments.

Figure 3-2. Sample Blended Design

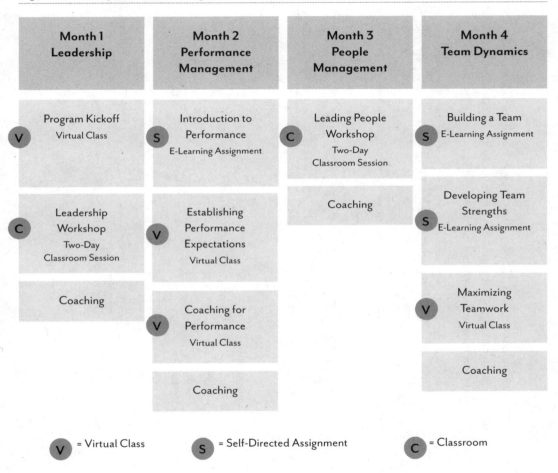

Tool 3-11. Sample Design Document

I create a design document to plan each learning event. This document describes each learning objective, the agenda topics, the online activity, and how much time it should take. Here is a sample design document from a one-hour virtual training class on using a financial system. Notice how the learning objectives are listed first, and then the topics, activities, notes, and time.

Objective	Topic	Activity or Learning Method	Materials and Notes	Time (minutes)
Engage participants from the moment they log in to virtual classroom.	Benefits of topic	Poll question: Which benefits will be most useful?		
Create a comfortable learning environment.	Welcome and facilitator introductions	Discussion		
Introduce participants and create community.	Participant introductions	Annotate: Click on map to indicate names and location	Slides	5
Establish expectations.	Logistics and ground rules			
	What to expect during today's session (agenda)	Whiteboard activity	Whiteboard	2
Access system using menus.	Selecting option on menu	Demonstration and lecturette		2

				Time
Work with existing accounts per established guidelines. Overcome common challenges of working with accounts.	Quick review of new screen. Actionable columns to filter. Small group activities	Screenshot with animated fill-in-the-blanks to show three new features. Poll questions. Two or three scenarios to filter (call on participants to ID scenarios). Small breakout group discussions. Discussion debrief with large group	Handout with blanks. Polls created in advance. Slides with participant annotation. Breakout groups. Whiteboards	10 / 15
Enter new accounts.	Review of new fields	Application sharing		5
Use the account approval process.	Workflow of approval process	Slide annotations	Handout with blanks	10
Make use of help screens.	Where to access the online help system	Audio clip	Upload audio	6
Create call to action for implementing new skills.	Close session	Insights and actions	Whiteboard	5
				Total Tme: 60 minutes

Tool 3-12. Design Document Template

Use this blank design document template to sketch out your virtual training class, then as a blueprint for development. Start by listing one learning objective per row, and be sure to leave space for an interactive opening and compelling close.

Objective	Topic	Activity or Learning Method	Materials and Notes	Time (minutes)
				Total Time:

Tool 3-13. Putting Together the Facilitator Guide

Once the design documents have been created and signed off on by all stakeholders, it's time to begin development. The next chapter of this book will focus on development; however, it makes sense to consider how the materials will be developed while you're still in the design stage.

The facilitator guide should include all virtual platform setup requirements, expected activity timings, discussion questions, and any other necessary information to effectively deliver the program. It should also include directions for the producer to co-facilitate or run the technology behind the scenes.

Here is a sample of my favorite style of facilitator guide to create for virtual training programs. Note that the facilitator notes are on one side of the page and the producer notes are on the other. Also note that slides—when used—are displayed on the page. When alternate activities are used (polls, whiteboards, and so forth), those items are displayed in the visual area.

Facilitator Notes	**10 Minutes**
WELCOME participants to the program. If bandwidth allows, consider turning on your webcam during your introduction to briefly give learners a snapshot of you. Turn off the webcam after your introduction.	
INTRODUCE yourself to the group. Include the following information:	
· your name and location	
· your role, major responsibilities, and experience.	
HAVE participants introduce themselves using chat, sharing their name, their role, and the time they have been in their current role.	OPEN an "Introductions" slide that has photos of the facilitator and producer on it.
· Comment on introductions as appropriate. Encourage participants to chat with one another.	INTRODUCE yourself both verbally and in the chat pod.
· Move quickly through the introductions. Remember that they have already met in the virtual academy, so this is just to encourage interaction in this session.	ENSURE handout is uploaded into a file share pod for those who need it.
ASK learners to download and print a copy of the handout if they haven't done so. Draw their attention to the file share pod where this handout is uploaded.	LET learners know you're available to assist with technical issues, and how to reach you both inside and outside the classroom.
SAY:	ASSIST with activity as needed.
It looks like we have a group who is ready to learn! We will continue using the chat window, as well as the status indicators and verbal dialogue throughout today's session. Your active participation is both requested and required!	SWITCH to "Orientation" layout before moving to the next slide.
· If needed, review how to use the status indicators (raise hand, agree, disagree, etc.) and how to send public and private chat messages.	

I use different facilitator guide styles for different organizations and situations. Some facilitators are used to a scripted guide, some prefer bullet point notes, and still others want a combination. Figure 3-3 is a facilitator guide sample that illustrates a scripted approach. Notice how the setup instructions are at the beginning, a start-before-the-start activity is included, and the producer notes are in sidebars along the left margin. You can download these pages at www.cindyhugget.com/actionguide.

This style of facilitator guide is helpful when a virtual training program will be run by multiple facilitators, and consistency for each delivery is important. Because the facilitator notes are scripted, the learners should have the same experience regardless of who is delivering the session.

Figure 3-3. Sample Facilitator Guide 2

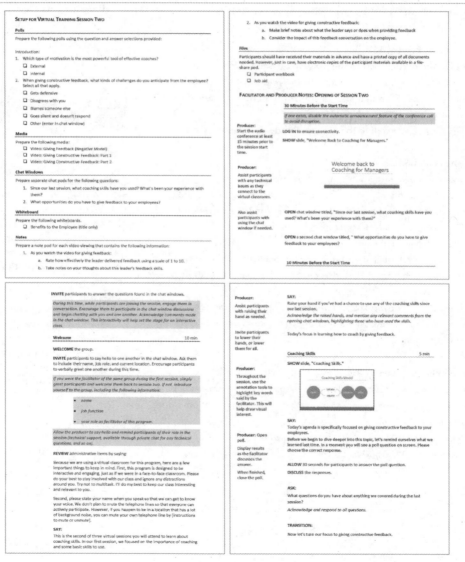

Tool 3-14. Tips for Creating Participant Materials

Many people are surprised to hear that I recommend creating and distributing participant handouts for virtual training classes. Some of them assume that electronic programs only need electronic resources, and therefore participant materials aren't necessary.

Another false assumption is thinking that the program visual aids (that is, the slides) make for good participant handouts. In fact, the best slides make the worst handouts because well-designed slides include only graphics and lean text, while the best handouts include reference material that can (and will!) be used back on the job.

Here are four reasons to include participant materials, and a bonus tip to keep in mind when creating them.

1. Participant materials serve as a reference guide for learners back on the job. The information can be a useful resource for remembering a process or walking through a new skill. Job aids, reference material, and other helpful tools should be included in participant handouts.

2. Having participant materials gives you another opportunity for learner engagement in the program. Participants can be asked to complete a short worksheet and then raise their hand on the virtual platform when finished. Or participants could be asked to do a fun scavenger hunt through the materials to find answers to questions. The possibilities are endless when you get creative with the handouts.

3. Distributing participant materials can help indicate to learners that this will be an interactive training program, and not just a passive learning experience. It can add a professional touch (especially if you use your organization's branded materials). It can also send the subtle yet essential message that thought and planning has gone into the program.

4. Participant materials can include virtual classroom activity instructions, which will reinforce the directions shared by the facilitator. For example, if a small group breakout activity is planned, the participant handout could include case study notes for the activity. Or if a role play is part of the design, the handout could provide the role-play instructions.

Handout Tip

If you plan to distribute participant materials electronically and ask the learners to print them, then be mindful of the document format. Consider the number of pages they will have to print, how much ink needs to be used on a page, whether participants will need access to a color printer (to understand a relevant graphic), and whether the information will actually be used during the virtual class. It's frustrating to learners, not to mention inconsiderate, when designers forget to look at the materials from the participant's point of view. Below are examples of a well-designed handout (left) and a poorly designed handout (right).

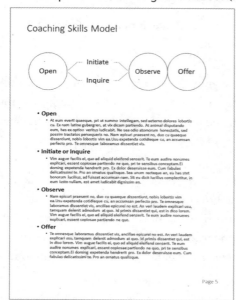
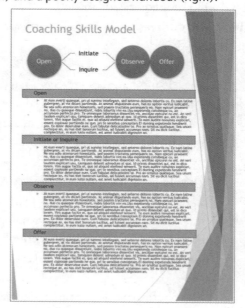

Tool 3-15. Designing for Webcasts

While most of this chapter has been devoted to designing interactive virtual training classes, for some learning objectives, a presentation-style webcast could be effective. You might have a topic where awareness is the goal and therefore an informative presentation is enough. For example, when one of my clients needed to educate their sales team about a feature upgrade to one of their products, they chose to disseminate this information in a live event. A skilled facilitator presented the information while engaging the remote sales team members through poll questions and chat dialogue.

If you are planning a presentation-style webcast, here is a sample session agenda that can be used to ensure it has at least some interactivity. This outline is similar to the 60-minute webcasts that I present to very large audiences. Note that even though this is a presentation, it still has interactivity and online dialogue threaded throughout. A template for your own use is also included.

Sample Webcast Agenda

Objective or Topic	Activity or Learning Method	Time
Engage participants from the moment they log in.	Have a topic-related question posted onscreen; ask attendees to respond to it in chat.	Before start of event
Spark interest in the topic with an opening statistic or quote	Ask attendees to react to the onscreen statistic or quote in chat.	2 minutes
Review agenda	Ask attendees to vote on their topics of interest using status indicators. Also ensure that attendees have handout (use file share if needed).	3 minutes
Introduce first topic	Use drawing tools to highlight key areas of the slides. Ask attendees to submit questions throughout; respond as they are asked.	8 minutes
Review question 1	Poll question and discussion of responses.	5 minutes
Introduce second topic	Use drawing tools to highlight key areas of the slides. Ask a thought-provoking verbal question at least half-way through this section; ask attendees to respond in chat.	8 minutes
Review question 2	Poll question and discussion of responses.	5 minutes

Objective or Topic	Activity or Learning Method	Time
Introduce third topic, preferably using media (i.e., video or audio clip)	Use drawing tools to highlight key areas of the slides. Ask a thought-provoking verbal question at least halfway through this section; ask attendees to respond in chat.	8 minutes
Review question 3	Poll question and discussion of responses.	5 minutes
Question and answer segment	Respond to questions that have been submitted; ask attendees to submit any remaining questions.	10 minutes
Wrap-up and next steps	Provide links and other topic-related resources.	5 minutes
		Total Time: 59 minutes

Session Planner for Webcasts Template

This is a fill-in-the-blank version.

Objective or Topic	Activity or Learning Method	Time
		Total Time:

Tool 3-16. Designing for Hybrid Programs

An increasingly common question asked by organizations is, "What about hybrid classes, where some participants are together in the same room and others are distributed remotely?" The trend of hybrid programs is growing, partly due to more readily available technology and partly due to increased comfort levels with videoconferencing. Almost anyone with a smart device can initiate a video call to connect with people in remote locations.

My first response to this question is don't do it. Avoid using hybrid audience programs when possible, because it's two different types of classes combined into one. It's partly an in-person program and partly a virtual program. In this type of learning environment, some participants will be able to write on the virtual whiteboard while others can't. One group can use the keyboard to type in chat, while the other cannot. One group can see each other's facial expressions, while the other can't. And so on. In addition, the facilitator gets pulled in two different directions and will either consciously or unconsciously focus on one group instead of the other.

Despite these limitations and my recommendation to avoid, it's still a noteworthy trend and one that should be addressed. Therefore, I asked my colleague Katie Stroud to share her experience in designing and delivering virtual training to hybrid audiences. Here's her take on it.

Design Tips for Sessions With Hybrid Audiences
By Katie Stroud, Co-Founder of Incremental Success

The in-person training experience is different from the online training experience—for the facilitator and the participants. And when these two experiences are combined, the difference becomes even more noticeable.

Developing instructional materials and designing for delivery always requires careful planning, but even more so when the participants are both on-site and remote, often called a hybrid audience environment. With a hybrid audience, some participants attend in-person (such as from the HQ office) with the facilitator, while other participants attend remotely (such as in the field or from different office locations).

Is It the Only Option?
If you find yourself being asked to design virtual training for a hybrid audience environment, the following tips should help you get started.

The need for hybrid training delivery grows as corporate expansion and mergers create teams spread across multiple locations. Technology has advanced to the point where remote collaboration is easier and more cost-effective. The temptation in training is to follow suit and facilitate training from headquarters while inviting remote participants to call in.

Before agreeing to develop or deliver training in a hybrid setup, consider whether other options exist. Some factors that might play into your decision include the critical impact of the training, budget in terms of both financial and time resources, the timing of the training, the number of participants in local and remote locations, and the potential for an ongoing need for hybrid training.

Critical impact: How important is the training program? While we might argue that all training is important (or else why would we be spending time on it), the truth is that some training has a bigger impact than other training. Will the training program save lives or prevent debilitating financial loss? If so, consider reaching everyone the same way, whether online or on-site, so that you can focus on the very important details necessary for achieving the training objectives. Ideally, the training's impact warrants enough budget for travel of either the participants or the facilitator.

Budget: The available financial budget may dictate whether you can cover travel for on-site training only. However, if you don't have time to prepare for hybrid training, could the learning participants be better served by a purely online training? Online training takes more design and preparation time as well, but may be more efficient than planning a hybrid solution.

Timing: When is the training class needed? Is there a high-profile release on the horizon that warrants training support teams before release? While gathering everyone locally and getting remote people online for the same training is tempting, failure to properly prepare for a hybrid delivery can leave remote participants feeling left out. If time is limited for delivery, consider pulling budget for travel to get everyone trained on-site or plan for an effective online delivery to reach everyone equally in time.

Participants: How many people need to be trained? How many people are on-site and how many are remote? How dispersed are the remote people? For very large populations or collective local populations with several scattered remote people, a hybrid solution might be ideal, especially when a permanent strategy is in place to support hybrid delivery.

Continued offerings: Does your training population include a large enough local audience to justify holding an in-person program? Or would a small number be better off staying at their desks as if they were remote? Or are there other reasons where support for hybrid training might benefit your organization? If such a strategy is already in place, then by all means, make use of the option as needed. If your organization needs a hybrid solution now and in the future, then take steps to implement a permanent solution.

Consider Outsourcing Facilities

Corporate offices increasingly include rooms designed for hybrid meetings. These meeting rooms include a large screen that everyone in the room can see, along with cameras and microphones designed to capture an audiovisual (AV) feed of people on-site for those attending remotely.

As advanced as these facilities are, the setup may not fully support the level of engagement needed in training. In addition, technical support for dealing with technical issues usually comes from someone in IT who is more familiar with servers and not necessarily AV equipment.

Outsourced facilities designed for hybrid training are often better equipped to support the facilitator and participants. In fact, these professional facilities pride themselves on producing a seamless experience so the facilitator can focus on engaging the participants.

Design, Design, Design!

If designing for the best learning experience in local or online facilitation is important (and it is), then designing for a hybrid experience is at least twice as important. Activities for local engagement need to be redesigned for remote engagement, but activities for engaging everyone locally and online require a strategy that works in both environments given the available tools and support.

For example, I was in a training session recently that used a card game to demonstrate the pitfalls of teams and silos. In this activity, the room was divided into three teams. The goal was "for each team to earn 21 points." Naturally, each team developed a strategy to reach 21 points first and "win." But the goal was to collaborate and help one another so that everyone would reach 21 points.

Simulating that experience online would depend on the tools available. The strategy might involve using virtual breakout rooms to allow each team to determine their strategy. But how would you divide the participants who were dispersed between local and remote locations? How would you have them "lay down" their cards? How would you offer the ability to collaborate among all participants? The answer involves getting very creative with the available tools and then testing your theories about how it should work in real time.

Prepare, Prepare, Prepare!

Whether you deliver training to a local group or to remote participants, preparation and rehearsal is vital. The technology involved in facilitating an online experience requires more time for preparation because you're facilitating from a technical cockpit. Hybrid facilitation is like facilitating from the captain's chair on a spaceship while you trust someone else to navigate so you can coach your crew to carry out a strategic operation with crewmembers on other ships. Planning for at least one rehearsal is vital. Extra time should be worked in for adjusting tools and logistics. The opportunity for additional rehearsals and coaching should be considered depending on the nature of the training session, experience of the trainer, and quality of the training materials.

As an instructional designer by trade, I often develop the materials and train the trainer on how to deliver them. This task used to be simple until I started designing materials for trainers to deliver online. The experience is different enough that trainers are often reluctant to adapt to the unfamiliar format.

In my first hybrid assignment, I set the expectations for a different experience and scheduled a rehearsal with the trainer. One rehearsal was not enough in this case. The rehearsal helped familiarize the trainer with the materials and he went on to practice on his own. On training day, however, he facilitated like he was reading a script and the training fell flat. He didn't engage with anyone beyond answering questions. While the instructional materials ended up surpassing the client's expectations, the participants would have benefitted from a better-facilitated session. Set expectations in advance and plan for plenty of coaching and rehearsal.

Defining Roles

Facilitating hybrid training requires a team of at least two, but usually more. The facilitator needs to be free to deliver the content and interact with the participants.

For smooth facilitation, at least one other person should be available to handle technical issues. In addition to tech support, having someone to help with remote interactions can help remote people feel included. In situations where at least some of the remote attendees are grouped together at a remote location, a co-facilitator and secondary technical support can add to the experience and further prevent technical snares and lonely remote participants.

As the instructional designer, I sometimes take the role of remote interaction manager. You may have seen this role labeled as "host." In a typical webinar, the host often reads an introduction and any obligatory details such as, "This session is being recorded." The host then steps aside and returns at the end to close with final details. But in training, remote interaction managers instead open with an engaging exercise to familiarize everyone with the tools and interactive format of the session. For example, they might tell everyone to "use the chat feature to tell us about your pets or a favorite pet story." They manage introductions and stay involved throughout the session, calling out remote participants by name and connecting them with the facilitator and other participants as needed.

In one hybrid session, I was the facilitator with a small group where three of the 15 participants had called in. I filled in as remote interaction manager for myself. Using names and talking to callers as if they were in the room set the example for other participants and soon everyone seemed to be engaging the callers as I had been. Eventually, the two participants who were serving as tech support also began supporting me in making sure our callers were invited to participate and their questions and concerns were addressed. Our callers added so much to the session. Without getting them involved, we would have missed some important learning opportunities.

The Small (but Significant) Things

Don't forget to plan for the logistics of taking breaks, distributing handouts, calling on people, displaying content, and sharing any AV feeds simultaneously. You will need to know the tools ahead of time to plan for these details.

For example, how does the tool show you that a remote participant has a question? Is there a raise hand feature? If so, how will the facilitator be notified? Do the remote participants know how to use the feature? Is the audio equipment sufficient for making on-site participants easily heard by remote participants? While taking breaks, will the AV feed be left on? Is there a way for on-site participants to connect with remote participants during a break? Will participants need to use their computers? If so, how will you manage computer activities and how will remote participants complete any computer tasks while staying connected?

The more attention you give to every single detail, the more effective the training experience will be. The best way to discover these logistical details ahead of time is to use the facilities and tools to deliver rehearsal sessions—more than one if possible.

Tool 3-17. Sample Session Planner for Hybrid Audience Program

If you must deliver virtual training to a hybrid audience (as described in this chapter), use this template as a session planner.

Topic	Activity for In-Person Audience	Activity for Online Audience	Notes

---

In Action: Hybrid Learning at Choice Hotels

"Our target audience is geographically dispersed. We are always looking for the right technology to use for learning events," says André Gratton, training manager for Choice Hotels. "We hold an annual convention for our learning team, and it can be a challenge for everyone to make it. So we piloted a hybrid event . . . some [participants] live in-person and others remote at their home location. Using the Citrix GoToTraining platform, we were able to have a live audience to use their own devices and made sure there was enough bandwidth available in the room, which allowed everyone to have a similar experience. We shared slides, used poll questions, chat, and had a producer who helped. It's important to us that a platform can work on different devices and provides the flexibility we need. We plan to use hybrid audience programs for all of our future conventions."

Summary

Once you have determined and documented your learning design, it's time to begin developing activities. With this foundational blueprint, you can get your creative juices flowing and enjoy the process of creating a high-quality, highly interactive learning event. Chapter 4 will show you how.

CHAPTER 4

Develop Activities

Once a virtual training design is established, then the program is ready for development. In most traditional instructional design models (such as ADDIE), a design document gets created first, and then the program development begins. The design document outlines the program components, indicates which exercises will be done, and establishes the overall flow of the activities. The design document serves as documentation for necessary sign-offs among stakeholders. It also becomes the essential guide for the next instructional design phase: development.

During development, the design springs to life. Activities are fleshed out, role plays are scripted, scenarios are written, and materials get created. Think of it this way: If design is the big picture, then development is the details. And if design is the whole-house blueprint, then development is the construction and interior decorating.

All the above is true for every instructional design project—whether you're creating a traditional classroom program, self-paced e-learning program, or blended curriculum. So what's different about developing virtual training? Mostly, it's the amount of interactivity required to make the live online event successful. Developing virtual training requires a different mindset about participant engagement. It also requires a new look at how to incorporate the virtual training platform tools into activities.

Remember, our definition of virtual training means that the learners are individually connected from geographically dispersed locations. They stay at their desks or some other remote location when connecting into the virtual training event. Therefore, their learning environment may be much less than ideal. There will be distractions all around them. They will be tempted to multitask throughout the event, either by checking their email or planning to get other work done during the same timeframe.

Therefore, interactive program design and fast-paced activity sequences are keys to success. The program must be designed in ways that keep participants' attention and engage them in learning. Instructional designers must keep this fact in mind when developing activities for virtual training classes.

Reasons for Interactivity

Let's explore the importance of interactivity even further. In addition to the challenge of distracted learners, engaging program designs lead to better learning results. To put it simply, learner involvement and engagement make for a better learning program. It's not engagement for the sake of engagement. Someone mindlessly clicking on the screen to select the green check button isn't likely to result in behavior change in the workplace. But if someone actively engages in conversation with their online peers from around the globe on a relevant training topic that has immediate workplace impact, then that's more likely to lead to the desired learning outcomes.

We know—both intuitively and from research—that adults learn by doing. An active experience is much better than a passive one. Think about yourself—how do you best learn? If you're like most people, you would rather get your hands on a new device and start playing with it than sit and listen to someone lecture to you about it. Or, you might be able to read about the new device in a book, but it won't be until you experience using it that you truly "get it."

Of course, there is a time and a place where lectures or reading books are the best method for a specific lesson learned. I'm not saying that lecture is never appropriate. But the best learning happens—the best behavior change happens—when participants get involved and get to practice.

This key fact is even more true in the virtual classroom. One of the greatest benefits and challenges of virtual training is that learners don't have to leave their workspace to attend. Virtual training *must* be more interesting and engaging than whatever distractions surround the participant. And while the virtual facilitator plays a role in making the program appealing to the learner, it's the training design that matters most.

Setting the Stage for Interactivity

The interactive nature of the training design should begin well before the program start time. Designers need to include robust program descriptions that pique interest and entice learners to pay attention. Registration messages need to set expectations that the program will be interactive. Reminder notes need to invite learners to take action in preparation for their learning. All these preprogram communications are created by the designer. Instructional designers—those who craft the structure and know the training best—should be the one writing these messages and including them in the program documentation.

In addition, as soon as participants log in to the session, they should be warmly greeted and invited to join an activity. By design, interaction should start when a person enters the virtual room. I call this the start-before-the-start time. It's a soft opener that sets the stage for what's to come in the rest of the session. Again, this welcoming activity comes from the instructional designer during the development process.

The tools section of this chapter includes many ideas on how to capture attention in advance of the program and engage learners upon login.

Continuing the Journey of Interactivity

Once the stage is set for learners to expect interactivity, the promise needs to be delivered on. Otherwise learners will tune out, and your program will not achieve its stated learning results. If you say a program will be engaging, then it's important to engage from the start and continue the engagement throughout the entire program.

A virtual training program design should include the start-before-the-start activity, an opening activity, and then interactivity at least every four minutes throughout the program duration. So if you do the math, that means a one-hour virtual training class should have approximately 15 engaging activities, not including the opener or prestart activity.

If your immediate reaction to that statement is, "But I have too much content to engage learners every four minutes!" then either you have a presentation-style webcast, or you need a new mindset about how to design virtual training activities. A webcast should still be interactive, but it serves a different purpose than a virtual training class. Remember, the goal of a webcast is simply to disseminate information, while the goal of a virtual training class is to achieve learning results and behavior change. And regarding a new mindset about designing virtual training, this chapter will help you with many tools, techniques, and ideas.

Why every four minutes? Consider your learners and the distractions around them. The program activities should keep their attention captured in the virtual training platform so that they learn the content and can apply it back on the job. Many virtual training experts use the every three-to-five-minute rule as a guideline based on both experience and research. I base my recommendation on research from Bob Pike (2002, 2011) and John Medina (2008), as well as my own experience of more than 15 years designing and delivering virtual training programs. Participants need to continually interact to stay engaged and not be distracted.

Platform Tools + Your Creativity = Interactivity

The good news is that most virtual classroom platforms provide a multitude of features that allow participants to meaningfully interact in ways that lead to the learning outcomes. Learners can talk to one another verbally or through chat. They can respond to questions in a poll, by writing on whiteboards, or typing their answers onscreen. They can get into small breakout groups for role play and skill practice. As Ruth Colvin Clark and Ann Kwinn wrote in their book, *The New Virtual Classroom*, "Virtual classroom software tools actually offer instructors more opportunities for frequent learner interactions than do most traditional classroom settings. Frequent and effective use of these response facilities is the single most important technique for successful virtual events" (2007, 107).

Interactive designs come from finding creative ways to use the platform tools in ways that drive learning and skill building. Therefore, instructional designers must be well versed in all platform features. When developing activities, they will combine their knowledge of the tools with their creative ideas to involve participants in the learning.

For example, let's say you are converting a management development program from in-person to virtual, and one of the learning objectives is to conduct effective performance review conversations. In the original course, participants role-play several scenarios to practice the new skill. In the virtual course, a designer has many options to choose from. Participants could practice the skill in many ways, such as getting into breakout groups to role-play the scenarios. They could also see the scenario description onscreen and discuss in chat. Or, they could respond to a series of poll questions related to the scenarios, or brainstorm scenario solutions on a whiteboard. And so on.

The designer looks at the learning objective, thinks about the best way for the participants to learn it, and then gets creative to develop an exercise that leads to the learning outcomes.

In Action: Advice From a Virtual Training Designer

I asked an experienced virtual training expert, Kassy LaBorie, to share some insights for developing interactive live online events. She has more than 16 years' experience in designing and delivering virtual training programs, and is the co-author of *Interact and Engage: 50+ Activities for Virtual Training, Meetings, and Webinars.* Here is her advice.

To ensure virtual training is interactive and engaging, make a commitment to focus on the active participation of the attendees rather than just the content of the program. Far too many virtual training programs fall prey to "must include all this content in an hour" syndrome. This leads to trainers who lecture, slides full of too many words, and a lack of meaningful activity to assist in the learning process. In our book, *Interact and Engage!*, Tom Stone and I compare engaged participants and disengaged attendees, as shown in Table 4-1.

Table 4-1. Engaged Participants vs. Disengaged Attendees

Engaged Participant	Disengaged Attendee
Focused and attentive	Uninterested
Active	Passive
Enthusiastic and eager	Bored and frustrated
Spontaneous	Reactive
Curious and inquisitive	Indifferent
Asks questions	Goes through the motions
Willing	Resistant

Source: LaBorie and Stone (2015). Used with permission.

But how do you create interactive and engaging virtual training? What does that look like for the instructional designer? Simply follow these three simple yet strategic steps.

First, clarify the program goal, and the individual objectives that participants will complete to meet it. What is the point, and what will participants do along the way to demonstrate they have learned it? The objectives answer the question of what it looks like to meet that goal, so ensure that they are actionable objectives.

Once the actionable objectives are clear, ask yourself: Which of those are social, or best learned with other people participating in the learning process? Virtual training sessions do not keep participants engaged when they are longer than a few hours or lecture heavy. To create an engaged participant, choose the social objectives for the live online training and allow the other objectives to be included in alternative learning formats such as asynchronous activities, discussion boards, reading assignments, and videos.

And then it gets fun! The third step is to map the social learning experiences to the features of the live online, synchronous platform. Use the whiteboard to share reactions to a new process, use chat to dive deeper into why those reactions influence behavior, go back to the whiteboard to discuss and identify productive behaviors, and then break out into teams to create an action plan to recognize reactions and begin to control behaviors and guide them to desired outcomes. There is no requirement to design a breakout or poll when focusing on the social learning of the participants. The features help participants demonstrate the objectives; all you need to do is learn what features you have available and how they work to create the engagement that participants have always wanted!

Tips, Tools, Templates

Developing activities is as much art as it is science. For many designers, the development phase is the fun part of creating a training program. The tools, checklists, and templates that follow will give you—the designer—ideas to create interactive virtual training programs that engage your participants.

Tool 4-1. 5 Reasons to Develop Preprogram Content

A virtual training program's interactivity should begin well in advance of the program start time. Participants form impressions about the program by reading its description, upon receiving registration information, and in the days leading up to the program. It's a ripe opportunity to prime the pump for interactivity. It gets the conversation started, so that the deeper dialogue can happen during the actual program.

Therefore, during the program development, you should create components for this often-overlooked part of the participant experience. Craft a thoughtful program description that emphasizes the participants' active role in the learning journey, and carefully consider all the ways the participant experience can be enhanced even prior to the official program start time.

In chapter 6, there are several example templates for pre-session communication messages. For now, here are five reasons why you should pay attention to the preprogram participant experience.

1. **Set expectations**. By describing the virtual training program with word choices such as *interactive, engaging*, and *active participation,* you'll begin to plant the seed that this program may be different from what they're used to. If you don't tell them it's an interactive training class, they'll probably think it's another lecture or conference call. Mitigate this potential problem of mismatched expectations by providing clear, descriptive information in advance.

2. **Build rapport.** By creating standard, scripted messages that a facilitator can use in advance of the program, you allow facilitators to connect with participants and become familiar with them. This is an important component that helps participants realize they will be interacting with a person and not just a computer screen. It sets the stage for interactivity.

3. **Create community.** If the learners are asked to connect with one another in advance on a shared platform (such as a discussion board), they'll begin to create networks and discover they are in a shared experience. Again, this component subtly helps participants realize that they will not be alone with a computer screen, but instead will be with other learners.

4. **Respond to questions.** Participants often have questions about the content or program in advance. Accurate, detailed descriptions will either mitigate or eliminate many of the program uncertainties. Participants will show up in a better state of mind if they know what to expect regarding program content and logistics.

5. **Set learners up for success.** Advance communication can build excitement for a program. It can also help create the right expectations and let participants know what they should do to be ready for a program. Do you need them to print a handout? Then communicate that in advance. Do you expect them to have a

headset so they can have hands-free typing? Then tell them that in the program description. Do they need to reserve a private conference room so that they can freely talk about sensitive subjects during this program? Then warn them in advance. All these seemingly small details can be important factors to participant success, so it's vital to include them in the preprogram communication.

Tool 4-2. Start-Before-the-Start Activity Planner

When does a virtual training program begin? For participants, their learning experience starts the moment they log in to the virtual classroom. (Of course, it can easily be argued that their experience begins upon program registration, but for the purposes of this section, we'll focus on participant login.)

Ideally, participants will join the event at least five to 10 minutes early, so that they can get connected, get settled into the classroom, and be ready to begin at the program start time. If your participants log in just at the start time, or past the start time, consider how you will communicate with them in advance and what expectations are set. Do they view it as just another meeting? Or as a training class? Would they be late to an in-person class? Are they used to facilitators waiting for everyone to join before starting the program? Getting participants to show up on time or early is part of a mindset shift about virtual training, and covered in more detail in chapter 6.

Just like a traditional training class, the virtual classroom should be welcoming, preparing the participants for the program that's about to start. In an in-person classroom, this might mean charts hung on the wall, tables set with participant materials, appropriate music playing, and a facilitator who greets everyone. In the virtual classroom, this means a rotating set of slides with class information, participant materials available for download, and greetings from the producer or facilitator. In addition, the virtual classroom must have an "attention-grabber" that involves the participants right away. You don't want them logging in and then tuning out, going back to their email, or whatever else they could be doing. And as we've already discussed, you want to make sure they know that they are expected to be an active participant.

If your learners are brand new to the virtual classroom, this start-before-the-start activity should also involve learning the basic platform features. If you'll be using poll questions, then have an introductory poll question onscreen when they log in. If you'll make use of chat, then ask them to introduce themselves in chat, which not only teaches them how to use chat but also gets the conversation going. If you'll need them to use the drawing tools for whiteboard activities, then display a graphic that requires them to point, click, and annotate. These types of activities serve a two-fold purpose: to get the participants actively involved and help them learn the platform tools. Of course, there's no need to do all these activities before the program start; just select the one or two tools that will be used first.

One more distinction to note: The start-before the-start activity could be either a standalone icebreaker or a topic-connecting opener. An icebreaker helps participants get to know one another and form social connections. It may or may not have anything to do with the program content. On the other hand, a topic-connecting opener is directly related to the content that will be covered during the program.

For example, if you post a photo of a world map onscreen and ask participants to mark their current location and introduce themselves, that's an icebreaker. But if you post a quote related to the program topic and ask participants to agree or disagree with it and explain why in chat, then that's an opener. Both icebreakers and openers can be useful as attention-grabbing activities.

I prefer to start with a topically relevant opener instead of an icebreaker because I don't want participants to get the false impression that we are only playing games and not here to learn. However, most virtual classroom platforms allow for multiple onscreen activities at once, so if I use an icebreaker activity during this time, then I'll also include an opener. See Figures 4-1 and 4-2 for two examples of start-before-the-start activity screens.

Figure 4-1. Start-Before-the-Start Activity Sample 1

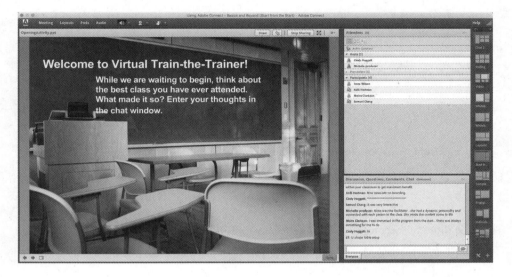

Figure 4-2. Start-Before-the-Start Activity Sample 2

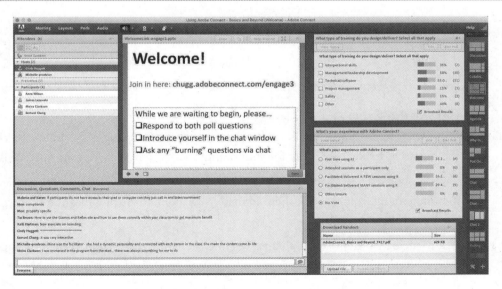

Finally, while the start-before-the-start activity gets participants engaged right away, it should not penalize those who arrive on time. It shouldn't be used to teach an important learning concept that won't be covered again in the program. Nor should it be a prerequisite for the program. It's simply a method to set the stage for interactivity, keep participant attention, and engage those who have joined early.

Worksheet: Start-Before-the-Start Activity Planner

1. What type of start-before-the-start activity do you want to plan?
   - ❏ Icebreaker
   - ❏ Opener
   - ❏ Both

2. What is your training topic?

3. What virtual classroom tools will you have available on the opening screen?

4. Slide share (either static or rotating, to share information)
   - ❏ Chat
   - ❏ Poll
   - ❏ Whiteboard
   - ❏ Drawing tools
   - ❏ File share (to distribute handouts or reference material)
   - ❏ Other:
   - ❏ Other:
   - ❏ Other:

10 Start-Before-the-Start Activity Ideas

Still wondering what to ask participants to do when they log in? Consider the following list and select the ones that make most sense for your event, or use them to spark your own ideas.

- Show a photo of a map and ask participants to use the drawing tools to mark where they are joining from. Or, ask them to mark their hometown, or a location they'd like to travel to for vacation.

- Ask participants to introduce themselves in chat, listing their name, their location, their job role, and a piece of personal information (such as their favorite hobby or the last book they read).

- Post a checklist of tasks, which include searching for virtual classroom tools (for example, "find and click on the raise hand button") and getting ready for the program (for example, "turn to page 3 of the handout").

- Invite participants to chat with one another. Ask them to talk about hobbies, family, work experience, schools, sports—anything that will help them find common connections. If they quickly complete this task, have them continue until they've found at least five (or more) things in common with the entire group.

- Post a thought-provoking question or quote that's related to the program topic. Ask participants to react to it using the status indicators, and to type responses in chat.

- Post a list of "sentence starter" phrases and ask participants to complete each sentence in chat.

- Use poll questions to ask participants questions about their experience with the program topic.

- Have a game board onscreen (such as a crossword puzzle or brain teasers) and ask participants to join in the fun. Even better if the game is related to the program (such as using program terminology for the puzzle).

- Post trivia questions related to the program topic. Have fun seeing who can guess the correct answers.

- Ask participants to introduce themselves by drawing a stick figure self-portrait of themselves on the whiteboard (Figure 4-3).

Figure 4-3. Stick Figure Introductions Activity

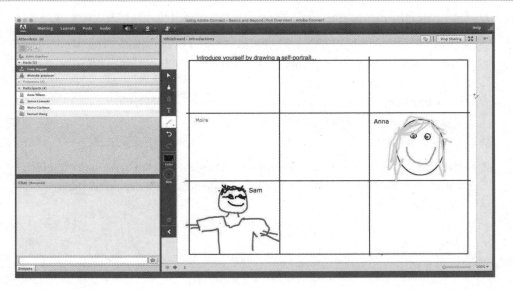

Tool 4-3. Planning an Opening Activity

Equally as important as the start-before-the-start activity is the initial opening activity. It should begin at the exact virtual training program start time. The opening activity should be an interactive exercise, as opposed to a facilitator spending 10 minutes explaining what to expect and how the program will be interactive.

5 Opening Activity Ideas

Here are some of my favorite opening activities:

- Reveal the program agenda in a poll question and ask participants to select which topic items are of most interest. This activity serves both as the agenda review and gets everyone involved at the same time.

- Post a whiteboard and have participants type in their questions about the topic. This activity helps a facilitator connect the program content to immediately relevant questions. It can also serve as a reference throughout the program.

- Ask a series of experience questions with status indicators (such as raise hands or green check/red x). This activity helps the facilitator get to know the audience, and the participants to get to know one another.

- Share a short, relevant case study onscreen and ask participants for their reactions to the scenario. It's even better if this scenario continues throughout the program, with references to it during other activities and exercises.

- Post a checklist of applicable common challenges and ask participants to choose which ones they can relate to. Use these challenges as conversation starters throughout the program.

> ## A Common Mistake
>
> I recently coached an instructional designer who was creating her first virtual training program. She wanted to make it as interactive as possible for the learners. She added in several poll questions, a whiteboard activity, and scenarios for skills practice to the 90-minute program. But the first activity didn't show up until about 15 minutes into the event. The facilitator would get to this first activity and wonder why no one was participating. The designer needed to add more interactivity at the start of the session. That way, when participants were asked to contribute in the first exercise, it wouldn't come as a surprise.

Opening Activity Planner Worksheet

Use this sheet to plan your opening activity.

Learning Objective or Topic:

Virtual Classroom Tools Used:

- ❏ Slide share
- ❏ Chat
- ❏ Poll
- ❏ Whiteboard
- ❏ Drawing tools
- ❏ Other:

Activity Description:

Tool 4-4. Outline: Welcome Message From a Senior Leader

For some virtual training programs, it helps to have a senior leader from the organization intro-duce the program. The leader could join in the class for the first few minutes live, or attend virtually by prerecorded video. When a senior leader welcome is used, make it as interactive as possible by providing a listening guide in the handout, or by asking learners to listen for a specific point that will be discussed as a large group afterward.

This introductory activity should be kept short, in proportion to the length of the overall program. In other words, if it's a one-hour virtual training event, then the welcome message should only be a few minutes long. In addition, I'd position this activity after an interactive opening, so that participants don't immediately tune out thinking that the entire program will be lecture based. Facilitate the icebreaker or opener, and then present the senior leader introduction.

Some topics, such as learning about a new organization-wide initiative, lend themselves well to this activity. But in other programs, such as a system update training program, it may not be necessary. Potential discussion points include:

- Welcome the group to the training program.

- Explain why participants were selected for this program. Were they nominated for it? Selected by their job role? Some other reason?

- Put the program topic into the context of the bigger organizational picture. Why this program? Why now? How does it fit into other programs or initiatives?

- Share what results the organization or business unit expects to achieve as a result of the investment in this training program. Emphasize the senior leaders' support of this program.

- Explain the "what's in it for me?" benefits of the program. In other words, why is this program relevant to participants? How will it help them do their jobs better?

- If virtual training is new to the organization, include information about the delivery method (that is, the organizational benefits of virtual training).

- Set expectations for participant engagement during the program. Mention the importance of paying attention and staying immersed in the content.

- If appropriate, mention the credibility of the facilitator delivering the program. Why is the facilitator the best person to lead the learning journey?

Tool 4-5. Developing Activities for Virtual Training Classes

Developing activities for virtual training classes essentially boils down to using the platform tools in creative ways that lead to the learning objectives. Here are a few ideas on ways to use some common tools for learning outcomes. Each tool is discussed in detail in chapter 2.

Activity Idea List for Each Common Virtual Platform Tool

Tool	Sample Activity Idea
Chat	Pair up participants and invite them to have a private discussion about a training topic. Then ask each pair to report one or two highlights from the discussion.
Annotate or draw	Draw a line that divides a slide (or whiteboard) in half. Have a relevant discussion topic that could easily be argued for or against. Ask half the audience to write pros on one side, and the other half to write cons on the other side.
Whiteboard	Ask participants to collectively design and draw an image that relates to the training topic, which will help them remember lessons learned.
Status indicators	Pose a challenging question, asking participants to respond using a status indicator. For example, they can use a green check for "strongly agree" and a red x for "strongly disagree."
Raise hand	Ask participants, "Who's ever experienced XYZ? Please raise your hand." Then invite each person to share a brief synopsis of the experience either verbally or in chat.
Polls	Create a competition by assigning point values to correct responses for each poll question. Run the competition throughout the virtual event, asking questions that check for knowledge transfer.
Breakouts	Divide participants into small groups and place them into breakouts. Have each group brainstorm solutions to a common challenge and report on their recommendations.
File or material distribution	Post a scavenger hunt list, asking participants to search for things in their handout. The first person to raise their hand indicating they've found everything wins a fun "virtual" prize (such as bragging rights).

Tool 4-6. 5 Energizer Activity Ideas

Energizers are short activities that capture (or recapture) participant attention at various points throughout a virtual training program. They are typically used after a break, after an intense dialogue, after a reflection activity, or just when a change of pace is needed. Energizers may or may not specifically relate to the training topic, and they usually only take a few moments to facilitate.

Here are five ideas for energizers:

1. **Brain teaser or trivia question.** Post a fun question onscreen and have participants respond through chat, poll, or status indicators. This could become a series of questions that are asked periodically throughout a program, with points assigned for each correct answer.

2. **Creativity challenge.** Open a whiteboard and ask participants to get creative. Assign a drawing (such as "family beach scene" or "life on a farm") and let them have a few moments of fun.

3. **What's outside your window?** In chat, ask participants to share one thing they see outside their window (or would see outside, if they had a nearby window). This activity is especially good right after a break, as everyone is transitioning back to their computer screens.

4. **Chair yoga pose.** I'm a registered yoga teacher, and one of my weekly classes is chair yoga for seniors. I sometimes incorporate a quick and simple chair yoga pose into the middle of a virtual class to help everyone stay attentive or release tension. For example, I'll ask participants to put both feet on the floor, sit up straight, and take a deep breath. Or I'll ask everyone to put their hands on their shoulders and draw their elbows backward, which opens the chest. These quick but meaningful movements can help everyone regroup and refocus.

5. **Photo puzzle.** Post a photo onscreen and ask participants to identify it. The photo could be a close-up of an everyday object that's not readily identifiable (such as a zoomed-in photo of the edge of a paper clip). It could also be a photo of a company building that not everyone would immediately recognize (for example, "That's our country headquarters in Brazil!"). The key is to use a photo that would pique curiosity among participants and give them a chance to guess what it might be.

Tool 4-7. 10 Tips for Incorporating Media Into Virtual Training Design

It's common to play media clips—prerecorded audio or video—in training classes to help participants learn something new. The same is true in virtual training classes, especially if the program is converted from a traditional in-person class. When using media in the virtual class-room, designers need to build in a few extra components to ensure the activity runs successfully.

Here are my top 10 tips for incorporating media into your virtual classes:

1. Because sound from the media clips typically plays through the participants' computer speakers, include this information in the pre-event communication. Let them know in advance that speakers will be needed.

2. Play a music clip during the start-before-the-start activities to allow participants to check the volume levels of their computer speakers.

3. Include instructions for the facilitator or producer—whoever sets up the virtual classroom in advance—to load the media clip into the platform (instead of relying on desktop or screen sharing). Also, if the platform has settings or preferences for media playback, include the recommended ideal settings in the facilitator guide notes.

4. Include instructions for the facilitator or producer to mute participant phone lines just prior to the media start, and to unmute them when the media finishes.

5. If the media needs time to buffer onto participant computers, provide talking points for the facilitator during those few moments. That way, participants won't notice the short delay.

6. Have a "listening guide" or set of questions for participants to consider while viewing the video or listening to the audio. These targeted questions tell participants what to focus on. Have them posted in chat or on a slide, so they are visible during the media playback.

7. Because the media will most likely play at different speeds on participants' computers, include instructions for participants to raise their hand when the video or audio clip finishes playing for them.

8. Link to the original video in the program materials, in case facilitators or producers need to alter the media clip into a different format for playback. Some platforms play FLV files, others need MP4, and other formats may become common in the future.

9. Offer a plan B in case there are any challenges with the media playback. For example, include a printed script of the text in a PDF format that could easily be distributed to participants if needed.

10. Add an introductory slide for the media activity that explains what will happen and any action needed by participants (Figure 4-4).

Figure 4-4. Video Tips

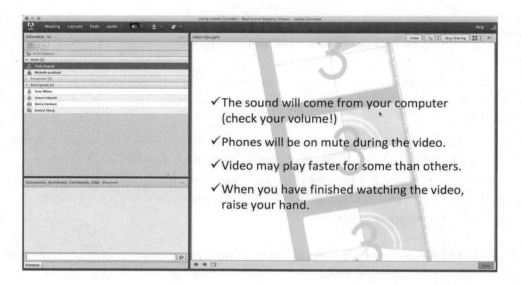

Tool 4-8. 5 Closing Activity Ideas

The main purpose of a virtual training class is to achieve the stated learning outcomes. We design and develop programs to impart knowledge, teach new skills, and help learners apply these new behaviors back on the job. Therefore, designers should plan for a closing activity that takes place at the end of a virtual event. This activity lets participants reflect on what they've learned and plan for how they'll take action after the program. Just like the opening of a training class is a key point in time, so is the closing of one. The closing activity leaves a parting impression and is the springboard to the next step in their learning journey.

Here are five ideas for closing activities:

1. **Share insight.** Ask participants to share one key insight they've gained during the program. Ensure that everyone participates by using a whiteboard with marked location for each person (Figure 4-5).

2. **Accountability pairs.** Have participants select a partner from the attendee list (or assign them), and use private chat to exchange contact information and arrange a follow-up conversation to discuss how they are applying the topic learned.

3. **Art gallery review.** Open a whiteboard and ask participants to take one minute to draw a picture of something they learned during the program. Anything goes, from stick figures to more elaborate drawings. Then ask participants to review one another's artwork (asking for descriptions as needed!).

4. **Note to self.** Ask participants to send a private chat to the facilitator, including their email address and a short note to themselves that they'd like to receive in the future. The facilitator would then save those notes and send them a few weeks after the program finishes.

5. **Red light, yellow light, green light.** Use a slide or whiteboard divided into three sections labeled "red light," "yellow light," and "green light." In the red section, ask participants to list anything that will stop them from implementing lessons learned. In the yellow section, ask them to list any potential roadblocks. In the green section, ask them to list any action items or ideas they have for applying the content.

Figure 4-5. Whiteboard Example

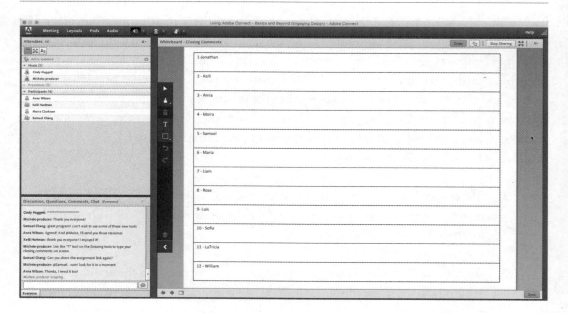

Tool 4-9. Worksheet: Questions to Ask When Creating an Activity

When brainstorming activities for a virtual training class design, ask yourself the following questions as a guide. These questions will help you think through which platform tools will be needed, what should be onscreen, and what corresponding information (if any) should go into the participant handout. They will also help you know what facilitator or producer instructions to put into the facilitator guide.

1. What's the goal of the activity?

2. What specifically will participants be asked to do? What platform tools will they use?

3. What do participants need to see onscreen at the beginning of the activity? In the middle of the activity? At the end or after the activity?

    Beginning:

    Middle:

    End:

4. What items (slides, polls, and so forth) need to be moved on or off the screen during the activity?

5. What activity instructions should the facilitator give verbally?

6. What's the producer's role in the activity?

7. How long should the activity take (in minutes)?

8. What else would be important to note about this activity?

Tool 4-10. Guidelines for Sequencing Activities in a Virtual Class

Once you've determined the virtual activities that belong in the program, it's time to review the sequencing. If you have developed the activities in linear order of the learning objectives and followed the blueprint set out by the design document, then your activity sequence is probably just fine. But there are some special nuances to sequencing virtual programs that should be considered.

There are several methods for sequencing a learning event. You could organize the learning by order of tasks completed on the job, position the topics from simplest to complex, use a priority calculation, or employ some other method. Everything you already know about sequencing learning is still true because learning in the virtual classroom is still learning. Yet the virtual classroom is unique. Assuming that the topic sequencing makes logical sense, here are a few questions I ask when reviewing a virtual training design. Note that by *tool*, I'm referring to the virtual platform features, such as chat, polls, raise hand, status indicators, whiteboards, and breakouts.

Sequencing a Learning Event Worksheet

1. Was the best tool chosen for each learning topic and activity? Is there a better option?

2. What variety of virtual classroom tools are used in the design?

3. Is the same tool being used over and over again? Or is there enough variety to maintain interest?

4. Are all the available tools used? What tools are missing from the design? Could they (and should they) be added?

5. Are the selected tools compatible with participant proficiency and comfort? For example, if everyone is brand new to the platform, then it may make sense to use polling instead of breakouts at first.

6. What order are the tools introduced in a program? I prefer to start with simple tools and then gradually get more complicated, especially if participant proficiency with the platform is unknown. For example, I'll start with the status indicators and chat, and then introduce drawing and whiteboard tools.

7. Are the tools used enough? Remembering the every-four-minute-guideline, does the program design contain enough interactivity?

Tool 4-11. Guidelines for Creating Slides for Virtual Training

A chapter on developing virtual training activities wouldn't be complete without a discussion of slide design. Slides are visual aids that assist with learning and a key component of most virtual training class materials.

However, slides should not be the main focus of a virtual training class design, like they are in a presentation. Instead, slides should serve the following purposes for virtual classes:

- Assist in making a point by providing visual or graphic illustration.
- Provide reference information.
- Show activity instructions.
- Provide context for a learning topic.
- Maintain participant interest by showing them something visually stimulating onscreen.

If you equate virtual training design and development to slide design and development, then you are heading down the wrong path. Developing a virtual training program is not "sitting down to create a slide deck for my presentation." Slide development plays a supporting role in the development process. It's one step—albeit an important one—to creating an effective virtual training program. But it's not the only step. Please don't confuse slide design with training design.

Note also that you will develop more slides for a virtual training program. If you compare the number of slides in a traditional in-person training program with the number in a virtual class, the virtual class slides will probably be double, for many reasons:

- Virtual class slides need to provide extra information that may not be needed in an in-person program, such as technical or activity instructions.
- Because participants are easily distracted, frequently changing slides onscreen helps maintain visual interest.
- Only one idea per slide should be shown onscreen.
- Some virtual classroom platforms don't allow for animation, or "build" slides. The workaround is to create one slide per animation.

A guideline for all slide creation, and an especially important one for virtual classes, is to use bullet points sparingly. Gone are the days of heavy, text-laden slides. There are so many other ways to display information than as an unimaginative list of text. You can replace bulleted lists with graphical displays, images, or a series of slides with keywords. If you must share a lot of text or other complex information with your participants, then use a reference guide, job aid, or other handout. See Figure 4-6 for an example of a list slide and an alternative way to display the content.

Figure 4-6. Slide Design Before and After

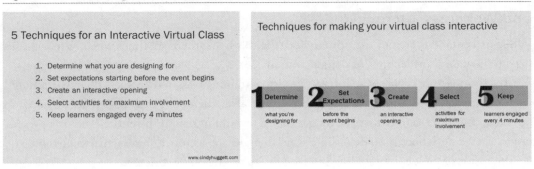

Slide Design Tips From an Expert

To help you create the best possible slides for your virtual training classes, I reached out to a noted expert in visual presentations, Wendy Gates Corbett. Here are her tips:

- **Use big visuals.** Make sure your visuals are large enough to be easily seen by participants. Keep in mind that participants may also have the participant panel or other virtual classroom features taking up screen space, so visuals on slides may end up smaller than you expect.

- **Make sure visuals have "write space."** You may have heard of *white space* when it comes to slides—it's space around text and visuals that helps participants see both. *Write space* is similar, but named because virtual facilitators often annotate directly onto a slide in the blank spaces. If you plan to use the web platform's text tool to write on the slide, make sure the visuals you use have space for you to write big enough for participants to see. You'll want the write space to have a light background so participants can see your writing.

- **Minimize visual distractions by removing as much extraneous slide content as possible.** This may include logos, copyright and other disclaimers, and slide numbers. The slide template used by the marketing and sales department is probably not the right template to use for virtual classes.

- **Use color to indicate a "lane change."** A slide with a different color background, for example, can indicate that you're changing subjects or activities.

- **Draw a blank.** Visuals don't have to be photos or illustrations. You can engage participants with a simple onscreen statement that has one or two blanks that you or a scribe fill in with the text tool.

Source: Wendy Gates Corbett. Used with permission.

Tool 4-12. 7 Tips for Making Online Lectures, Presentations, and Webcasts Interactive

While presentations are not the primary focus of this book, there are times when virtual classes need to include short lectures or demonstrations.

If a short lecture is part of an interactive virtual training class and lasts less than five minutes, with an interactive session immediately before and after, then no special design action needs to be taken. But if the segment will be longer than a few minutes, or if the entire event is a presentation, then a developer should consider ways to make the lecture as interactive as possible.

Here are seven ideas for adding interactivity to online presentations:

1. Frequently ask participants to use their status indicators (that is, agree or disagree) to voice their current reaction to the presentation.

2. Use a fill-in-the-blank discussion guide handout, which asks participants to write in key words from the presentation.

3. Share an interesting, relevant story that captures attention. If appropriate, thread the story (or pieces of the story) throughout the presentation.

4. Ask thought-provoking questions throughout the presentation. For example, ask participants to share their biggest challenge they encounter when trying to apply the training topic.

5. Pair up participants, open private chat, and periodically ask them to briefly discuss a key point.

6. Use multiple voices (for example, a panel discussion or an interview-style format) to help maintain interest.

7. Use the shared notes feature of the virtual classroom platform to invite participants to take notes and share with the entire group.

Tool 4-13. Developing Activities for a Global Audience

Good virtual training design creates a highly interactive participant experience that is focused on learning outcomes. However, to appeal to a culturally diverse audience, factor in these five additional design techniques:

1. Recognize different perceptions about virtual training.
2. Allow for extra communication time during a session.
3. Use culturally neutral examples and graphics.
4. Choose scenario character names recognizable to a diverse audience.
5. Develop and send materials ahead of time to minimize potential language barriers.

Recognize Different Perceptions About Virtual Training

Different cultures have different views of training, which naturally transfer to perceptions of virtual training. For example, some cultures have an informal style and consider the facilitator a peer or colleague, which influences how they interact. In contrast, some other cultures view the facilitator as the expert and would not interrupt even if they had an important comment to share. They may hesitate to ask questions, or wait for an invitation to participate during a virtual session.

Therefore, use these techniques when designing a virtual training program for a global audience:

- Make it easy and comfortable for participants to speak up during class by establishing ground rules and setting expectations at the beginning of the event.

- Design activities that invite conversation in safe ways, such as using paired chat exercises and small group breakout rooms.

- Emphasize use of the chat feature for both public and private communication.

- Make liberal use of the status indicator tools for participants to voice opinions without actually using their voice.

Allow for Extra Communication Time During a Session

When a session is delivered in English to participants who speak English as a second language, or when multiple languages are represented during a session, extra communication time will be needed. The participants may need a few extra seconds to translate or mentally process an unfamiliar word, or to compose their chat response to a question. They also might need more time to read a poll question and all the choices before submitting their answer. These extra seconds add up to longer activity times and longer class times.

The design challenge with a mixed language audience is to not slow down the class too much, which could lead to a loss of interest from those who do speak the native language. If the timing moves too slowly to maintain their interactivity, they may lose interest and disengage from the session. The key is finding the right balance between too fast and too slow.

Use Culturally Neutral Examples and Graphics

When designing virtual training for global participants, pay attention to any cultural references that may deliberately (or even inadvertently) be included. An American football analogy may work fine for a U.S. audience, but global participants may not fully understand it. Designing an activity based on a popular U.S. game show could be fun, unless the rules are confusing to those not as familiar with it. Similarly, avoid pop culture references that won't be recognized by a global audience. Television shows, games, cartoons, and the like are all potential avenues for misunderstanding.

Even something as small as word choice can make a difference in comprehension and acceptance. For example, there is an activity I like to design into in my virtual train-the-trainer classes that illustrates how we give and receive instructions. I ask participants to take pen and paper, imagine they are at the office, and write down directions to their home for someone who needs to get there. (We then debrief how they wrote down the instructions—did they draw a visual map, list out step-by-step turns, or something else altogether?) The point in this example is the deliberate word choice of *to your home* instead of *to your house*. *Home* is a more generic, globally relatable term than *house*. In addition, take care with graphics, such as photos or vector graphics that may be included on a slide. Select graphics that will not cause offense or be controversial.

Choose Scenario Character Names Recognizable to a Diverse Audience

Similar to using culturally neutral examples and graphics, when writing role plays or case studies for virtual classes, select names for characters that will be recognized by a global audience. If it's an interpersonal skills course that will have a manager-employee dialogue to use during practice, choose everyday names for the characters. Also be sure to select a variety of names that represent multiple cultures. So instead of naming your characters traditional American names like Peter or Mike, you might select other names such as Pritha or Akido.

One of my favorite sources for finding names is to search the web for popular baby name lists by country. I especially like to select names that are popular in more than one language, such as Adam or Maria. Being intentional about your name choices will help localize the content and help participants relate more to the scenario.

Develop and Send Materials Ahead of Time to Minimize Potential Language Barriers

I recommend that participant handouts be included in every virtual training program, especially if the participants speak multiple languages. Create these reference materials and distribute them in advance. That way, participants have time to review any technical or unfamiliar words. Let participants know that the session will be conducted in English (or whichever language will be used). Include instructions for an extra pre-session assignment to review the handout so that participants can look up those words and translate them into their native language.

Likewise, when designing materials for global audiences, avoid jargon and spell out all acronyms. Finally, leave enough white space on each handout page so that participants have room to take additional translation notes.

Summary

The end of the development phase of any instructional design project—virtual training included—is the production of facilitator guides, participant materials, and any other resources deemed necessary to achieve the learning outcomes.

Once the program has been developed, it's time to facilitate it! The next chapter focuses on facilitator selection, preparation, and delivery techniques.

CHAPTER 5

Work With Facilitators and Producers

Successful virtual training programs are the product of two key components: interactive design and effective delivery. It takes both to create training programs that achieve learning results. Combined together, these two elements create a positive participant experience, which in turn enables participants to learn and apply new skills.

The previous two chapters focused on creating interactive designs. Once all aspects of the program development are complete, it's time to focus on the other key success factor: delivery.

Facilitators and Producers

Program delivery by skilled facilitators who engage remote participants using virtual classroom tools is vital to realizing learning results. But becoming an expert virtual facilitator takes more than just presenting content or reading online slides. Facilitators must connect with an audience they cannot see. They have to build rapport, teach concepts, check for knowledge transfer, and keep participants' attention, all while using the tools in a virtual classroom platform. They must engage remote learners in dialogue while maintaining a productive learning environment.

Successful program delivery also requires another key role—the producer. Expert producers manage the technology and ensure a seamless participant experience. Producers support the facilitator behind the scenes and sometimes even co-facilitate sessions. They often are the person who sets up the virtual classroom with slides, polls, breakout rooms, and other platform settings. Producers handle the technical details of virtual classes, and help keep everything on track.

The producer's role in the virtual classroom is similar to that of a radio talk show producer. The radio producer is the person who answers the telephone, keeps the show on time, and cues the commercials so that the radio show host can interact with call-in listeners and provide the show's main content. On some radio shows, the producer becomes part of the cast of characters and joins in the on-air dialogue. On other shows, the producer is never mentioned and stays behind the scenes. This is true in the virtual classroom as well: Sometimes the producer is an active, vocal part of the class, and other times the producer stays silent. Regardless, the producer's role is critical to the success of both a radio show and a virtual class.

The Benefits of Two Session Leaders

In a traditional in-person classroom, most training programs only have one facilitator. There may be supporting administrative roles that assist with pre-or post-class logistics, but the facilitator is the only one who interacts with participants and shows up to the classroom the day of the event. Therefore, the mindset of having two session leaders—a facilitator and a producer—in the virtual classroom requires a change in thinking for most training organizations.

The most effective virtual training programs have a facilitator and a producer, for several reasons. First, virtual training relies on the use of technology for learning outcomes, so it makes sense to have one person responsible for the learning and one person responsible for the technology. And while most virtual classroom platforms are stable and reliable, many other potentially unstable technology variables play a part in a successful program. Having a producer means that the facilitator can focus on the learning even if the technology doesn't cooperate. The facilitator can continue the program if participant needs extra assistance with their technology connections. Even if there aren't technical problems, the producer typically manages the platform tools during the class so that the facilitator can stay focused on the participants and their learning.

You can deliver a virtual training class with only one session leader. I have delivered more events than I can count without producer support. But it's not ideal; it increases the potential for technical disaster. If even one participant has technical difficulties that draw the facilitator's attention away from the rest of the group and the learning plan, then the ability to realize expected results will be jeopardized. Having a producer makes for a better participant experience.

If your organization wants to use virtual training because it's the best method for your employees to learn, and because your technology allows for it, then embrace the virtual training initiative. That means providing a producer for each program, so that you are truly investing in the participant experience. Producers help create a seamless virtual training experience for learners.

But if your organization incorrectly perceives a producer as an extra expense instead of a value-added necessity, then you may need to justify one. Build a business case for including a producer in the virtual training investment. Or, get creative in how you can supply a producer on a shoestring budget. The tools section of this chapter includes ideas for finding a producer.

Trainers, Facilitators, Presenters: What's in a Name?

So far in this chapter, I've referred to the virtual trainer as the *facilitator*. It's my preferred term for the learning leader because it implies responsibility for dialogue, not just a presentation monologue. I also use the term *virtual trainer* interchangeably. Your organization might use different terminology, and that's OK. Whether you call this person the trainer, facilitator, instructor, or some other name, this role is the leader of the virtual training session.

As mentioned earlier, effective facilitators enhance the experience for participants in a way that motivates them to learn. They ask questions to provoke thinking. They present content in easily understood ways. They give instructions to complete learning exercises. They encourage participation. And they create a comfortable, safe learning environment where participants are free to practice new skills. If those are the things your virtual trainer/instructor/presenter/facilitator is doing, then we are on the same page.

Likewise, *producer* is my preferred term for the technical leader. However, this person may also be called *host, moderator,* or *technology partner.* Again, the terminology isn't as important as the role itself.

Selecting Facilitators and Producers

When determining who will become a virtual facilitator, or when determining which external virtual resource to select, there are a few essential guidelines to follow.

First, remember that many of the best in-person classroom facilitators do not make the best virtual facilitators (and vice versa). It's like the common thinking that some television stars aren't the best radio show hosts and, in turn, radio stars don't always translate well on television.

This is because each medium requires a similar but different skill set. Many of the presentation and facilitation basics are the same, yet remote participants and technology tools require different competencies for successful delivery. It's like driving a car versus driving a bus. The rules of the road are the same but some of the techniques are different. In this chapter's tools section, you'll find a list the skills and competencies required for outstanding virtual facilitation.

Second, consider trainers' personal preferences. Some love the in-person classroom environment and want to stay there. They value the personal connections they make during the event. While it can be argued that these things are also present in the virtual classroom, they are not as plainly obvious. On the flip side, some virtual trainers are excited about the online classroom, such as using new technologies for learning and inviting a global perspective into a class discussion.

Third, outstanding virtual facilitators embrace technology and work well in a fast-paced environment. They master the ability to switch quickly between virtual classroom tools while monitoring participant engagement, leading a discussion around the topic, and anticipating the next activity. Yes, traditional classroom trainers also multitask behind the scenes, but there's an extra layer of effort when using technology as the main delivery mechanism. The best virtual facilitators possess this combination of technology savvy and quick thinking. So when selecting virtual facilitators and producers, look for this almost intangible but important skill. Check out the tools section for some interview-question tips and a list of skills to look for in your next set of virtual facilitators and producers.

In Action: Upskilling Facilitators and Moderators

Mars University delivers learning programs to its global community of 75,000 associates. Some of the challenges they face are reaching their associates in more than 200 locations across 74 countries, the timing of when programs are needed, and limited delivery resources. After exploring a variety of options, they determined that a solution of blended and virtual learning programs would help them meet this challenge.

The team began the process of selecting a platform, designing programs, and considering deployment managers. They needed to upskill a group of facilitators and moderators who could deploy and deliver these new virtual programs. Even though the team was highly skilled in traditional classroom rollouts, they recognized that to effectively implement virtual programs, new skills would be required.

Their first step was to identify and upskill an initial group of online moderators. (They deliberately chose the title *moderator* instead of *producer* because the role would include overall responsibility for blended curriculums and not just producing live online events.) They selected a specialized group of regional training managers who are responsible for program implementation in their respective geographic areas.

I partnered with the team to create a customized train-the-virtual-moderator curriculum for the candidates. We helped them learn the new processes, platforms, and producer skills that would be needed for live events. Over the course of several weeks, they attended meetings, training events, and practice sessions to learn the new skills. Global Supply College Manager Jessica Pyle said, "We knew that having highly skilled moderators would be a key success factor, so we wanted to be sure they were fully prepared."

In parallel, the first set of virtual facilitators was also selected. Because the moderators would take responsibility for communicating with participants, managing the blended program learning components, and running all technology for the live online events, the facilitators were subject matter experts and business unit leaders who occasionally delivered learning programs in their local regions. Therefore, the facilitator upskilling program focused on platform basics and the specifics of what's the same and what's different when facilitating online. The new virtual facilitators learned and practiced the skills of engaging remote audiences with dialogue and the platform tools.

As a result of the targeted upskilling process, the Supply College within Mars University had a prepared team of moderators and facilitators when the first virtual programs were ready for global deployment. The new programs were met with overwhelmingly positive feedback from associates who appreciated the ability to participate virtually. The bottlenecks to program delivery were minimized, and virtual learning is now rapidly expanding in scope and reach.

Tips, Tools, and Templates

The rest of this chapter is devoted to tools, templates, and checklists that will help virtual facilitators and producers prepare for and deliver high-quality virtual classes.

Tool 5-1. Reference Chart for Virtual Training Roles and Responsibilities

Start by clearly defining and delineating roles and responsibilities in the virtual classroom. The chart shown contains typical responsibilities, but may not be true in every situation. For example, the producer typically runs the technology behind the scenes; however, skilled facilitators might choose to open their own poll questions during class.

Role	Typical Responsibilities in the Virtual Classroom
Facilitator	Also called trainer or instructor, this person delivers the training class and is responsible for explaining content, giving activity instructions, listening to participant comments, engaging participants to further learning, gauging knowledge transfer, and providing feedback.
Producer	This person is the technical expert who assists the facilitator. Some producers specialize in technology-only assistance (working with participants who need help connecting), while other producers co-facilitate sessions with the trainer. A producer may be called a host or moderator.
Coordinator	The administrative person who the handles logistical details of virtual training events, this person might also manage and maintain the organization's LMS, as well as communicate with participants before and after an event. The coordinator may or may not join the live event. If so, it's usually to take attendance or distribute electronic evaluation forms.

In Action: Roles and Responsibilities at Coventry Health Care

At Coventry Health Care, the training coordinator tasks are split between three people. Once a virtual training program is scheduled, each of the following individuals play a role in the program's success:

- The **learning consultant** performs LMS administrator tasks by setting up the course in the LMS and supporting the facilitator with any LMS needs. The LMS sends automated messages to participants upon registration, and reminders as the program date draws near. The learning consultant stays involved by monitoring the LMS inbox and responding to participant questions.

- The **facilitator** creates and sets up the online class, makes sure that participants have the virtual classroom links, and manages the roster and attendance reporting. Drawing from a set of standardized messaging templates, the facilitator communicates with participants before the program to set expectations and prepare them for learning.

- The **learning coordinator** awards continuing education units to participants based on what's been recorded by the facilitator. This important step occurs post-program, and gives participants the paperwork needed to maintain their professional certifications.

According to senior learning consultant Mark Aronson, "The facilitator owns the learning environment. Just as a facilitator would be responsible for setting up their own face-to-face classroom, so they are responsible for setting up the virtual classroom. They have support from learning consultants in the background, but ultimately it's the facilitator's role to take charge and create a positive experience for learners."

Tool 5-2. Comparison Between Traditional Classroom Facilitation and Virtual Facilitation

A common question from new virtual trainers is, "What's different about facilitating in the online classroom?" There are many similarities, such as the foundation of adult learning principles that transcend delivery methods. However, there are three key differences that virtual facilitators should note:

1. **Use of technology.** While classroom trainers should be versed in technology from their traditional in-person classes (projectors, slides, videos, etc.), in the case of virtual classroom training, technology takes center stage as the delivery method. Technology adds a layer of complexity to training delivery because learners are remote, connected using a web-based program, and often using their own devices.

2. **Need for updated skills.** When delivering virtual training, facilitators must draw upon a new and updated skill set. Notably, they need to make the most of their voice when speaking. Verbal and vocal techniques become especially critical when cameras are off and class discussion primarily uses audio. In addition, the most effective virtual facilitators are skilled multitaskers, needing to manage many aspects of virtual delivery at the same time.

3. **Engage learners in new ways.** While learner engagement is important in all types of learning, it takes on a new dimension in the virtual classroom. Because participants stay in their own workspaces, there's great potential for them to only partially pay attention to the learning event. They may keep their email program open, work on other projects, or simply be distracted by their surroundings. Therefore, it's essential for virtual facilitators to make extra effort to engage participants in their own learning. As outlined in previous chapters, the program design should be engaging, but so should the virtual facilitator. Additionally, facilitators have an entire virtual platform full of interactive tools available to create dialogue and enable learning.

Tool 5-3. List of Skills Needed for Virtual Facilitation

In my previous career roles as training manager and director of training, I hired many training professionals to deliver programs. I was always searching for candidates who had the perfect blend of presentation skills, technical proficiency, content expertise, professional presence, and the ability to connect with participants. Those competencies are still important to me when I look for effective virtual facilitators. Yet virtual facilitators also need some additional skills to be successful in the live online classroom.

Effective virtual facilitators possess a unique blend of training, facilitation, and technology skills. More specifically, they:

❐ Apply adult learning principles to the virtual classroom.

❐ Show that they are technology savvy (or willing to learn).

❐ Can engage an unseen audience.

❐ Make learners feel comfortable with the technology and the virtual learning environment.

❐ Multitask effectively.

❐ Have credibility with the program content.

Tool 5-4. Virtual Facilitator Job Description

If you are hiring a new virtual facilitator to join your team, or retooling your existing job descriptions to include virtual training skills, consider the following sample job description as a starting point:

- Delivers virtual training programs to remote audiences using {*insert name of virtual platform used by your organization*}.

- Collaborates with designers, SMEs, and stakeholders to gather relevant program information.

- Prepares for every virtual delivery.

- Meets with producers and co-facilitators prior to every program delivery to ensure smooth transitions and clear division of responsibilities.

- Uses a variety of facilitation tools and techniques to engage remote audiences.

- Presents information using a variety of instructional techniques or formats, such as role playing, simulations, team exercises, group discussions, videos, or lectures.

- Provides positive and constructive feedback to learners.

- Applies adult learning theory to all virtual training delivery.

- Stays current in virtual training trends and platform updates to continually deliver innovative learning solutions.

Tool 5-5. Skills Needed for Virtual Producing

The most effective producers are experts in the technology platforms used for virtual training events. They need to not only know the virtual training platform inside and out, but also have a solid understanding of computer hardware and software in general.

Other important qualities for virtual producers include the following:

❒	Problem solving and troubleshooting skills
❒	The ability to remain calm under pressure
❒	The ability to juggle multiple things at once
❒	The ability to think quickly and take action as needed
❒	The desire and willingness to keep learning
❒	The ability to follow instruction from facilitator and producer guides
❒	The ability to respond quickly to requests from the facilitator and participants

Tool 5-6. Interview Questions for Potential Virtual Facilitators and Producers

When interviewing potential candidates for a virtual facilitator or virtual producer role, consider including the following questions in your interview:

- What's your specific experience with interactive live online delivery (more than just putting presentations online)?

- What virtual classroom platforms have you used? How did you learn how to use them? Which one is your preferred platform and why?

- What's your experience delivering live online programs to a global audience? How do you factor in cultural differences to your delivery?

- How do you build rapport with remote participants?

- Tell me about a time when technology problems got in the way of learning. What did you do?

Tool 5-7. Ideas for Producer Resources

As mentioned, it's a best practice to have two session leaders for every virtual event—the facilitator and the producer. However, if having a producer isn't an option for you, here are some solutions to consider:

- Have a facilitator-in-training play the role of producer.

- Find someone in the organization who wants to learn more about technology and train them to be a producer.

- Have a partial producer, someone who joins the session for the first 10 to 15 minutes to help with the initial connectivity.

- Ask your platform supplier about technical support services offered, to see if they would provide in-session producer support.

- Partner with your IT department when scheduling classes, asking them to provide a producer resource during virtual training classes.

- Create a producer job role in your training department and have that person be your full-time producer for virtual training classes.

- Hire an external partner who will supply producers on a class-by-class contract basis.

Tool 5-8. Technology Checklist for Virtual Facilitators

When a facilitator prepares to deliver a live online event, use this checklist to prepare for technology requirements.

Hardware		
	❐	Computer or laptop
	❐	Second computer or laptop for backup purposes*
Software		
	❐	Required downloads or plug-ins for virtual platform
Audio		
	❐	Hands-free headset
	❐	Reliable telephone or VoIP connection**
Internet Connection		
	❐	Speed test for appropriate bandwidth as required by the virtual classroom platform and the program design—for example, whether or not live video will be streamed

* Facilitators should have two computer connections for two reasons; first, so they can view both the host or presenter login and the participant view. They need to be able to discuss and explain exactly what the participants see on their computer screens. Second, they should have a backup computer in case of technology failure or other glitch. This is especially important if they are without a co-presenter or producer. Ideally both computer connections are desktop or laptop computers, with the full software installation of the virtual program. If the virtual platform mobile app is different from the desktop version, the mobile device should only be used for emergencies.

** The facilitator may also need to plan for redundancies in telephony and possibly Internet connection in case of unexpected technical issues. For example, facilitators who work from a home office should have a backup telephone (such as a mobile device) and an alternative Internet connection (such as an air card or nearby Wi-Fi hotspot).

Tool 5-9. Tips for Learning Technology

How do you learn a virtual classroom platform? Here are several methods:

- Click on every button—try it!
- Read the help screens.
- Use online tutorials on the supplier website.
- Participate in user discussion boards.
- Attend sessions as a participant.
- Practice using it.
- Log in as a host and as a participant.

Checklist for Learning Technology Skills

When learning a virtual classroom platform, use this checklist to guide your progress.

Category	Tasks
Administrative Options	❐ Create the virtual classroom and generate links. ❐ Manage access and entry into meeting rooms. ❐ Install any necessary software and plug-ins. ❐ Configure classroom preferences (such as participant privileges). ❐ Set up audio connections (VoIP, teleconference, or both).

User Options	❐ Determine roles and permissions (host, presenter, attendee).
	❐ Use platform tools:
	    ❐ Attendee list
	    ❐ Chat
	    ❐ File share or file transfer
	    ❐ Notes
	    ❐ Share documents (such as slides or media files)
	    ❐ Polling
	    ❐ Whiteboard
	    ❐ Web links or content
	    ❐ Breakouts
	    ❐ Status indicators (raise hand, agree/disagree, etc.)
	    ❐ Video or webcam
	    ❐ Other:
	    ❐ Other:
	    ❐ Other:

Miscellaneous	❐ Know what the host, presenter, and participant views look like for each user option, such as which buttons and commands are available.

Tool 5-10. Setting Up a Virtual Facilitation Workspace

In preparation for a virtual class, facilitators and producers should think through and plan for their delivery setup. Just like classroom facilitators determine if their tables and chairs should be arranged in pods, chevron style, or U-shape, virtual facilitators should consider what equipment is needed and how it will be set up.

In general, a facilitator or producer delivery space should be a quiet spot that's free from distraction. It needs a solid Internet connection, preferably wired instead of wireless, to minimize any potential for interference.

Here are four common options for a virtual facilitation workspace:

1. Use your private office or room in your work building.
2. Create a shared virtual training room in your office.
3. Set aside a distraction-free workspace in your home office (Figure 5-1).
4. Establish guidelines for remote office, such as if you're working from a hotel room, shared office space, or other off-site environment.

Figure 5-1. Cindy's Virtual Facilitation Setup

Photo Credit: Emma Pilkington

Tool 5-11. The Extra-Prepared Virtual Facilitator and Producer Checklist

The original version of this checklist appeared in my 2010 book, *Virtual Training Basics*. It quickly became one of its most popular resources. Most virtual facilitators and producers recognize the need to prepare backup plans, just in case something unexpected happens. I equate being prepared to the way an Olympic athlete prepares for the games. It may seem like extreme preparation to some; however, it's taking the time to do everything you can do to be your best.

This checklist is designed to help virtual facilitators and producers prepare for an event in the way a world-class athlete would prepare for one. To use it, place a checkmark next to the items that are completely true for you. Then add up the number of checks in each section, totaling all checks for a final score. The scoring key is at the end.

Virtual Classroom Software

❏	I know the full extent of capabilities that the virtual classroom software has.
❏	When logged in as the host, I know what every button and every menu command does.
❏	When logged in as the presenter, I know what every button and every menu command does.
❏	When logged in as a participant, I know what every button and every menu command does.
❏	I am aware of all unique features of the virtual classroom software (for example, how many breakout groups can be used at one time).
❏	I know what file types are supported by the virtual classroom software's file-sharing feature.
❏	I have tested every feature and activity that we will be using in the virtual classroom during my training event.
	Subtotal

Internet

❏	I have a solid high-speed Internet connection in the location where I will be delivering virtual training.
❏	I have a backup Internet connection available in the location where I will be delivering virtual training.
❏	I have a second backup Internet connection available in the location where I will be delivering virtual training.
	Subtotal

Computer

❏	I have a reliable computer or laptop that I will use to deliver virtual training.
❏	I have a second reliable computer or laptop that I will use as a "sidekick" when delivering virtual training.
❏	I have another backup reliable computer, laptop, or tablet that I can use as a backup to my main or sidekick computer to deliver virtual training.
❏	All software, drivers, and plug-ins necessary to deliver virtual training are fully installed on all my primary and backup computers.
❏	All my devices and backup devices are powered on and ready to go prior to the start time of my virtual training event.
❏	All my devices and backup devices are fully charged and can run from battery power if needed.
	Subtotal

Telephony

❏	I have reliable telephone service that I will use when delivering virtual training.
❏	I have a backup telephone connection that can be used if needed (i.e., my main telephone is a landline and my backup telephone is a cell phone).
❏	I have a second backup telephone connection that can be used if needed (i.e., my main telephone is a landline, my backup telephone is a cell phone, and my second backup uses a different cell service provider).
❏	I have a compatible hands-free headset to use with my telephone.
❏	I have a backup compatible hands-free headset to use with my telephone.
❏	My telephone and all accessories I use have a clear sound connection (i.e., I can be clearly heard at all times when speaking).
❏	All backup telephones and accessories have a clear sound connection (i.e., I can be clearly heard at all times when speaking).
❏	My primary telephone headset is fully charged prior to the start of the virtual training event.
❏	All of my backup telephones are fully charged prior to the start of the virtual training event.
	Subtotal

Training Files

☐	I have a printed copy of every training file associated with the virtual training event (facilitator guide, participant workbook, saved poll questions, etc.).
☐	I have a second printed copy of every training file associated with the virtual training event.
☐	I have an electronic copy of every training file associated with the virtual training event that can be easily accessed from my computer.
☐	I have an electronic copy of every training file associated with the virtual training event that can be easily accessed on every backup computer, even if the Internet connection is down.
☐	I have an electronic copy of every training file associated with the virtual training event that can be easily accessed from any computer with an Internet connection (i.e., stored on an accessible website).
	Subtotal

Training Event

☐	I have all web links for my virtual training event, including host, presenter, and participant links if they are different.
☐	I have all event passcodes, including host, presenter, and participant codes if they are different.
☐	I have all teleconference details, including moderator and participant codes.
☐	I know all the teleconference commands for moderators (e.g., *21 to activate breakout groups).
☐	I know all the teleconference participant commands (e.g., *6 to mute and *7 to unmute an individual telephone line).
☐	I have all logistical details, including web links, passcodes, and teleconference information, printed out prior to the virtual training event.
	Subtotal

Facilitator Support

☐	I have a producer who will assist with all technical details of the virtual training event.
☐	I have a backup producer who could fill in for the producer if needed.
☐	I have another facilitator or trainer who could fill in for me at the last minute if needed.

❏	I have a second backup facilitator or trainer who could fill in for me at the last minute if needed.
❏	I have a technology specialist available to assist participants behind the scenes.
❏	A technical support person who is knowledgeable of the virtual classroom software and teleconference service is on-site or available at every location where participants are located.
	Subtotal

And because this is an extra-prepared checklist, here's a bonus section.

Participants

❏	I know the participants' full names and job positions prior to the virtual training event.
❏	I know the length of time participants have been with their organization.
❏	I know the length of time participants have been in their current role.
❏	I know the biggest challenges the participants have related to the training topic.
❏	I know the questions that participants will have related to the training topic.
❏	I know whether participants have talked with their direct supervisor about the training topic.
❏	I know whether participants will be held accountable for what they learn.
❏	I have personally spoken to or exchanged messages with each participant about the training event.
❏	I have verified that participants have completed all prerequisites or pre-session assignments for the training topic.
	Subtotal

Grand Total:

Scoring Key

60	Fantastic! Enter your name on the Extra Prepared Facilitator All-Star List!
50–59	Excellent! Consider helping other trainers learn from your preparation efforts.
40–49	Congratulations! You are extra prepared to deliver virtual training.
30–39	You are prepared, but have room for improvement. Select a few areas where you can improve your preparation.
20–29	You are on the verge of preparation. Identify the next five items you can add to your virtual delivery preparation.
10–19	You have started to prepare and have opportunity to improve. Select 10 items from this checklist that are most important for you and make an effort to add those to your list.
0–9	Ask an experienced virtual facilitator for assistance in getting started.

Tool 5-12. Checklist for Facilitator-Producer Pre-Session Rehearsal

It's both a best practice and common sense for the session leaders to connect and communicate in advance of a virtual event. The purpose of this meeting is to review the session outline, go over materials, determine exact responsibilities, and practice using the virtual classroom tools for all planned activities.

Review logistics and housekeeping to ensure consistency:	❏ Date ❏ Time ❏ Time zone ❏ Which platform? Which version? ❏ Link to session ❏ Host and administrative passwords

Practice the class:	❏ Discuss every activity and how it should work.
	❏ Confirm roles and responsibilities for platform features:
	  ❏ Polls
	  ❏ Whiteboards
	  ❏ Chat
	  ❏ Breakouts
	  ❏ Other:
	  ❏ Other:

Establish communication and emergency protocols:	❏ Decide how to communicate during class. (Private chat? Presenter-only-area notes? Other?) ❏ Determine what type of information should be communicated during class. (Timing reminders?) ❏ Determine backup communication channel. (Outside of the platform, such as text messaging?) ❏ Create backup and contingency plans for each activity.

Tool 5-13. Checklist for Facilitator-Producer Post-Session Debrief

At the end of each virtual event, the facilitator and producer should meet to review lessons learned and areas they can improve for next time. Use the following questions to guide this discussion.

1. How was the participant experience? What can be improved for next time to make things easier or smoother for participants?

2. Did each activity run as planned? If not, why?

3. Did the participants know what they should be doing at all times? Were any additional instructions needed?

4. How did the actual timing compare with the planned timing? Are there any adjustments to make for next time?

5. How could the facilitator-producer partnership be improved?

6. Were there any other lessons learned?

Interview With a Virtual Facilitator

I recently had the opportunity to connect with Lee Slimm, an independent training consultant who focuses on virtual delivery. Here's our exchange:

Cindy: How did you become a virtual facilitator?

Lee: After a nearly 20-year career in technology sales and sales leadership roles at companies ranging from startup to multinational, I was ready for a change. So I started a small voice-over practice, which is a lot of fun but was never going to be enough to pay the bills. A tennis associate of mine was working on contract virtual training engagement for a small Bay Area company named 3G Selling and suggested I get in touch with them because they needed additional resources. The rest is history!

Cindy: How did you learn the skills needed to be a virtual facilitator?

Lee: Initially I read every how and how not to whitepaper, book (including yours), articles, and so forth. I also believe the training I received in preparation for the voice-over work paid off. Once I was confident I could actually do the virtual work, most of my learning came from lessons learned, both good and bad.

Cindy: Let's assume it's a day that you're delivering virtual training. What does your day look like?

Lee: Since most of my work comes from time zones other than my own, a typical day usually involves an early wake-up. I require 60-90 minutes of mental warm-up and wake-up, so for a 6 a.m. Pacific session I am up no later than 5 a.m. I will drink some tea to warm my throat up and review the materials one final time. Thirty minutes before a session begins, I launch the virtual meeting room and audio bridge. This gives me ample recovery time should something not be functioning as expected, as well as prep time with my producer.

Immediately after the session ends, I will type up my notes, grab all the pertinent data from the meeting room, and submit all the administrative elements needed for record-keeping and billing purposes. If I am doing another session, it is almost a rinse-and-repeat cycle before, during, and after the next session.

Cindy: During a virtual event, what are some things you do to keep participants engaged?

Lee: Being mindful of the various learning styles that are out there, I try and include something for every style, such as videos and simple but interesting slides for the visual learner; music, voice inflection, and videos for the auditory learner; and chat entry, whiteboarding, and polls for the kinesthetic learners. I am also a big fan of directed questions early and often, letting folks know they need to be on their toes. Keeping a running track of whom I have heard from and whom I have not allows me to spread the attention and again allows for fewer chances for folks to disengage.

Cindy: What advice would you give to others who want to be a virtual facilitator?

Lee: While traditional classroom training skills are for the most part complementary to virtual skills, there are others needed like tech savvy, use of voice, and working from a tight script and not sounding like you are doing so. My best advice is to read as much as you can on the modality dos and don'ts and then work with an experienced virtual facilitator to practice and hone your skills. Their experiences will save you a lot of learning the hard way.

Tool 5-14. Get to Know Your Audience Worksheet

To plan out relevant stories and examples, virtual facilitators should research as much as they can about participants in advance of a class. Use this worksheet to help gather that information, and then use it to prepare notes.

1. Who are the participants? What are their names, roles, locations, or other relevant demographic information?

2. Do the participants know one another or are they meeting for the first time? If they know one another, what's their relationship? (Manager, employee, peers, other?)

3. What's the reason they are taking this class? What do they hope to gain?

4. What are their experience levels? Will the content be new information, or are they knowledgeable enough to be teaching the course? Or is it somewhere in between?

5. What types of questions might they have about the material? What concerns will they have? What challenges will they have in applying the content?

6. What is their level of experience with virtual training? Have they attended live online classes in the past? Are they already familiar with the platform?

Tool 5-15. Day-of-Event Planning Checklist for Virtual Facilitators and Producers

Some virtual facilitators think preparation for an online class is similar to preparation for a theater production: The stage is set, actors rehearse their lines, tickets are sold, and the show is ready for patrons. Likewise, a virtual class goes through a similar preparation process. This checklist, adapted from the *Infoline* issue "Simple, Effective Online Training" (Huggett and Corbett 2008), can help ensure that you are prepared for your next virtual classroom training event.

Participants have been sent:
- ❐ pre-work instructions installation instructions for virtual classroom software
- ❐ logistics such as links, passwords, and audio information
- ❐ participant materials to print
- ❐ contact information for questions or technical support.

Facilitator and producer have materials ready:
- ❐ slides
- ❐ facilitator and producer notes
- ❐ instructions for all activities and exercises
- ❐ contingency plans
- ❐ virtual classroom setup and materials uploaded.

Equipment is ready:
- ❐ Computers and equipment have been checked and tested.
- ❐ Applications and necessary files are open, available, and ready. All nonessential applications are closed.
- ❐ Audio technologies such as telephones or microphones have been tested.

Facilitator and producer are physically ready:
- ❐ Delivery area is ready (free of distractions, glass of water available, and so on).
- ❐ Training materials are readily available.
- ❐ Platform technology tools such as whiteboards and drawing privileges are enabled.
- ❐ Phone number and contact information for IT or vendor support is available.

Tool 5-16. Facilitation Techniques for Engaging Virtual Participants

There's both an art and a science to engaging remote participants in the virtual classroom. The "science" of engagement stems from the program design (was it created and developed with collaborative exercises that lead to the learning outcomes?), as well as the guidelines we established earlier about frequent interactivity. The art of engagement comes from the virtual facilitator's skill, technique, and style.

The Virtual Training Guidebook introduced nine engagement techniques for use by virtual facilitators. Here's the recap for reference:

Set Expectations

The most common complaint I hear from virtual facilitators is that participants don't engage, they don't respond, and they multitask during online classes. I firmly believe that the biggest reason for this problem is that proper expectations are not set in advance and at the beginning of class. Participants need to know and be held accountable for taking an active role in their own learning. Facilitators create an interactive environment by how they greet participants upon log in, set expectations for interactivity, and invite them to engage.

Build Rapport

Because virtual facilitators don't see participants face-to-face, they need to build rapport. They aren't presenters who read from a script; instead, they create dialogue and interact, which requires relationship building. Facilitators can do this by focusing on the learner experience, and remembering that it's about the participants learning and not about making a presentation.

Create Community

When remote participants join into a session, they often feel isolated. Yet a virtual class is a shared social experience with other learners in the same journey. Virtual facilitators should encourage participant interaction as much as possible, and as soon as possible, through dialogue and conversation.

Read Nonverbal Body Language

Despite the fact that most virtual classes don't use webcams for visual support, it's still possible for virtual facilitators to pick up on participants' body language. It's like the common thinking that you can hear a person's smile through the telephone; a skilled virtual facilitator can sense if a virtual class participant is engaged in the program. Participants express their nonverbal body language through their tangible participation in activities. In other words, you can see if they have typed in chat or responded to a poll question. They also express themselves through the frequency of participation and the quality of dialogue. If a program is interactive in nature, you should be able to tell which participants are following along with the content and which ones are struggling.

Use Platform Tools

Every virtual classroom platform has many tools and features that can be creatively used to engage participants. From creating a competition using poll questions, to assigning partners for a paired private chat discussion, to asking for frequent feedback using status indicators, facilitators can use all these tools to keep participants engaged. Participants should be clicking and typing and talking throughout the entire duration of a virtual class.

Share Only Relevant Examples

Virtual facilitators who do their homework can learn about the participants and then tailor stories and examples that make sense to them. The more relevant the content, the more engaged the participants, because they see value in it.

Use Your Voice

To help maintain interest and engagement, you need lots of energy and enthusiasm in your voice. Eliminate extraneous filler words, which are distracting. Speak confidently and conversationally. Pay attention to your pitch, speed, volume, and tone. It's difficult to listen to someone who speaks in a monotone voice, especially when it's already challenging to pay attention.

Multitask Effectively

The more you can effortlessly multitask during a virtual program, the more you can focus on participant engagement. In other words, if you are overwhelmed with keeping up with the technology, then you won't be able to keep up with the learners. But if moving from one task to another is comfortable and easy, then you will have the mental bandwidth to focus on learner engagement.

Manage Technology

Because virtual delivery relies upon technology, it's inevitable that there will be technology challenges along the way. Unfortunately, these challenges can interfere with participant learning and encourage participants to disengage. For example, if getting into a breakout group is cumbersome and the audio connections are choppy, then a participant is much more likely to disconnect and do something else. But if the technology works seamlessly and simply enables virtual learning to happen, then a participant is more likely to stay engaged. Virtual facilitators may not be able to control unexpected technology glitches, but they can control how they react to them and how they present solutions.

5-17. Virtual Delivery Tips for Success: A Quick Reference Guide for Facilitators

Facilitators can use this quick reference chart as a job aid while delivering a virtual session. Hang it in a conspicuous place (like a bulletin board) so that you'll easily see these reminders just before every virtual delivery.

❐	Create a comfortable environment for participants.
❐	Set ground rules and expectations.
❐	Help participants learn the software throughout the session.
❐	Give specific direction on how to answer questions. (Chat? Poll? Verbal? Other?)
❐	Keep the focus on participants throughout class ("guide on the side" vs. "sage on the stage").
❐	Minimize the impact of any technical difficulties.
❐	Be confident in your knowledge of technology.
❐	Create enthusiasm and excitement using your voice and attitude

Tool 5-18. Facilitator Considerations for Culturally Diverse Audiences

It's common for virtual facilitators to encounter an online classroom full of culturally diverse participants. The diversity could come from differences in geography, learning preferences, technology comfort, experience levels, or many other reasons. Because their main responsibility is to create a learning environment that helps participants learn and apply new skills, facilitators must recognize and accommodate these differences. So, to appeal to a globally dispersed and culturally diverse audience, virtual facilitators should pay attention to the following delivery techniques.

Create a Comfortable Learning Environment

It's always important to create an environment that's conducive to learning. However, a diverse audience will have differing expectations about their role as participants, so virtual facilitators need to take care to build rapport and establish participation ground rules at the start of a session. They should make everyone feel comfortable engaging with one another despite any language barriers. For example, a facilitator might invite participants to respond either verbally or in the chat window, whichever is their preference.

Virtual facilitators should inform learners up front about any participation expectations, such as "expect to be called upon during class." While calling on someone can help maintain interest and engagement, it can also embarrass someone who is reluctant to speak. So when using direct questions, the point should be to increase participation, not to put someone on the spot. Only use directed questions sparingly, and ones that do not have a right or wrong answer, like, "Sofia, what do you think about the process?" instead of "Sofia, what are the first three steps of the process?"

Use Clear Language

When participants speak a different language from the facilitator, it's extra important to use clear, concise language. This means that facilitators should take care to not use jargon or uncommon phrases, and to slow down their rate of speech. For example, the facilitator should say "use" instead of "utilize" or "buy" instead of "procure."

Also, when saying participant names during class, virtual facilitators should learn the correct pronunciation and use it. Ask for pronunciation help if needed. A trick I use is to phonetically spell out each person's name on a blank sheet of paper I keep on my desk. This helps me remember how to correctly say each name during class.

Recognize Cultural Differences

By its very nature, delivering virtual training to a global audience will reveal cultural disparities among participants. These can be as subtle as time zone differences or as magnified as how people interact in a breakout group setting. Virtual facilitators should watch for these nuances and ensure that they don't get in the way of learning.

For example, it's normal for a widely dispersed audience to be joining at different times of their day. Facilitators who only say "good morning" to everyone could immediately undermine their credibility if it's already afternoon or evening for most participants.

Tool 5-19. Developing Virtual Facilitators and Producers

Continuous improvement should be a common theme for virtual facilitators and producers. Use these observation forms to monitor performance, enhance and coach delivery skills, and provide feedback. There are two samples provided: one for a facilitator and one for a producer.

Virtual Facilitator Observation Form

Facilitator:	Class:
Observer:	Date(s) Observed:

Skills	Observed	Comments
Creates a comfortable learning environment	❏ Creates a welcoming online environment ❏ Adapts content to make it relevant to learners (uses stories, examples, etc.)	
Engages learners	❏ Invites learners into the conversation ❏ Creates opportunity for discussion and dialogue ❏ Draws out learners who are silent	
Asks questions	❏ Asks appropriate mix of questions (open, closed, overhead, directed) ❏ Gives instructions for how to respond to each question (poll, chat, raise hand, verbal, etc.)	
Facilitates	❏ Refers to, but doesn't read, slides ❏ Maintains a learner-centered mindset	
Builds rapport	❏ Shows interest in learners ❏ Uses learners' names ❏ Uses a conversational tone	
Makes the most of their voice	❏ Speaks clearly and audibly ❏ Conveys enthusiasm for the topic ❏ Sounds energetic and confident	
Uses technology effectively	❏ Uses platform tools ❏ Handles technology challenges with ease	

Additional Comments:

Virtual Producer Observation Form

Producer:		Class:	
Observer:		Date(s) Observed:	

Skills	Observed	Comments
General Skills	☐ Creates a welcoming online environment for participants and facilitator(s) ☐ Sets up the virtual classroom in advance per program setup instructions ☐ Constantly monitors what goes on during the session, responding quickly to all requests and needs ☐ Follows facilitator or producer guide for activities and directions ☐ Contributes to discussions and activities by offering references, comments, or other appropriate supporting information ☐ Helps participants with technical difficulties	
Technical Skills	☐ Demonstrates proficiency with basic platform features ☐ Gives instructions as needed for how to use platform tools ☐ Displays confidence with all tools in the technical environment ☐ Responds quickly to any technical problems that occur during a virtual event ☐ Remains calm when technical challenges arise ☐ Moves to backup plan as needed	
Partnership Skills	☐ Creates a seamless partnership with the facilitator for a quality learner experience ☐ Listens actively for cues from the facilitator ☐ Provides positive feedback to facilitator and participants as appropriate ☐ Invites learners to participate in the event	
Communication Skills	☐ Speaks clearly and audibly ☐ Gives clear and concise instructions ☐ Sounds energetic and confident	

Additional Comments:

Tool 5-20. A Facilitator's Guide to Responding to the Unexpected

Effective facilitators who prepare relentlessly will be able to quickly rely on their backup plans for any unexpected technology challenges. If they lose Internet connectivity, they switch to their backup provider. If they disconnect from the audio, they quickly reconnect. If an activity doesn't work exactly as they had planned, they respond with flexibility and switch to something else. Their backup preparation pays off in these situations.

When it's a different type of challenge, one that occurs unexpectedly or one that would not be prevented with preparation, then an effective virtual facilitator will still respond with ease. When unforeseen challenges arise during a virtual class, a facilitator should do one or more of the following:

- Stay calm and take a deep breath.
- Let participants know what's going on (if appropriate).
- Use backup plans.
- Spend just a moment or two troubleshooting.
- Take a short break to deal with the situation.

Even though producers are typically assigned the task of troubleshooting or handling any unexpected challenges that arise during class, a facilitator should also be prepared to deal with the unexpected.

Tool 5-21. The Skill of Multitasking

Most people agree, and headlines frequently report, that humans are unable to multitask. We perform best when focusing on one task at a time, and when we try to do more than that, we will actually perform worse on everything. I don't disagree with these research findings. Multitasking is difficult under many circumstances.

However, a small but significant percentage of the population has the cognitive ability to multitask without a drop in performance (Strayer and Watson 2012). In addition, there are many things that you and I do every day that would be considered multitasking. When we eat breakfast while watching TV and talking with our family, we are multitasking. And when we drive a car, we are simultaneously doing many things at once to get to our destination. These are just a few examples of common activities where we multitask.

As previously detailed in this chapter, multitasking while delivering a virtual program is an essential skill for both facilitators and producers. They must be able to encourage participant learning while running all aspects of the technology, and do everything in between. Most virtual classroom programs are like large equipment consoles, and facilitators need to keep their eyes on all the buttons.

The good news is that multitasking is a skill that can be learned and improved upon. It's a matter of preparation and speed, of mastering a skill so that you can do it quickly without giving it too much space in your brain's working memory. For example, think back to when you were first learning to drive. You had to slowly and deliberately complete each action required to start the car. Now, after years of practice, you start the car without much thought. Or, for instance, someone new to typing will hunt and peck for keys on the keyboard. But watch an experienced typist and you'll see fingers flying effortlessly as the words appear onscreen. In both cases, the task didn't change, but the person's practice and experience increased. The tasks still require thought and attention, but the level of cognitive processing required has decreased.

The same is true in the virtual classroom. The more a facilitator practices and prepares, the easier it will be to keep track of all the moving parts.

The following worksheet, from *Virtual Training Basics,* is a short self-assessment for facilitators, on how well they currently multitask. After, I've included a list of tips and techniques to use for better multitasking success.

Multitasking Checklist

Rate yourself on the steps for multitasking success.

	Never	Rarely	Sometimes	Usually	Always
I set myself up for success before the virtual training event.	1	2	3	4	5
I am completely prepared to deliver my training content.	1	2	3	4	5
I fully know the virtual classroom software that I will be using.	1	2	3	4	5
I have a producer or co-facilitator who will assist me during the event.	1	2	3	4	5
I can type quickly and accurately.	1	2	3	4	5
I have predefined "trainer pauses" identified (planned places in the program where learners are busy and I have a moment to regroup or review).	1	2	3	4	5
I am comfortable with my virtual training delivery skills.	1	2	3	4	5
I have eliminated all distractions from my workspace to focus on the virtual training event.	1	2	3	4	5
I am comfortable with letting unimportant things slide without comment in the virtual classroom.	1	2	3	4	5

What skills are already your areas of strength?

What skills will you focus on first to help you be a better multitasker when delivering in the virtual classroom?

7 Tips for Multitasking in the Virtual Classroom

These are tips I share with new facilitators who want to improve their multitasking muscles to enhance their virtual delivery. These specific actions help to free up your mind so that you can focus on the participant learning experience.

1. **Be prepared.** The more prepared you are, the less mental capacity you have to use thinking about other things. You won't worry about what's coming next because you'll already know it.

2. **Know the software.** The better you know the platform, the easier it will be for you to use its tools without much extra thought.

3. **Use a producer or co-facilitator.** The division of responsibilities and support available when there are multiple session leaders allows each to have more precise focus on their specific tasks.

4. **Be a proficient typist.** The faster you can type in chat and onscreen, the quicker you'll be able to move onto the next task. Also, you won't need to use up mental capacity trying to find keys on the keyboard.

5. **Practice, practice, practice.** The more you experience multitasking in the virtual classroom, the easier it will become.

6. **Resist temptation to do too much.** The recognition of what's possible versus what's too much for you to handle at any given time is important. For example, close out of your own email and clear your own desk of to-dos that could potentially distract your attention away from the virtual delivery.

7. **Know what's OK to let slide.** The feeling that you have to acknowledge every comment in chat, or respond to every virtually raised hand is a real struggle for some virtual facilitators who think they must do it all. However, there are some things you can let slide. For example, in a participant chat activity, you can often summarize all the chat comments with one statement instead of individually reading and talking about each one.

Tool 5-22. Vocal Warm-Up Exercises for Virtual Facilitators

Select one or more of these techniques to warm up your voice prior to delivering a virtual training event.

- Quietly hum your favorite song.

- Slowly say the alphabet vowels (a-e-i-o-u). Exaggerate your facial expressions while doing so. Repeat in various vocal tones (low, medium, high) and in various volumes (soft, medium, loud).

- Sing the musical scale (do, re, mi, fa, sol, la, ti, do) forward and backward several times in a row.

- Open your mouth as wide as you can and say "ahhh" (as if you were in the dentist chair). Close your mouth, and then repeat.

- Warm up your facial muscles by pursing your lips together (like a kiss) and then smile wide. Go back and forth between these mouth positions.

- Warm up your neck muscles by gently looking side to side, and then up and down.

- Shrug your shoulders up and down while taking in deep breaths. Breathe in as your shoulders go up, and breathe out while your shoulders go down.

- Stand up and read aloud a few sentences from your favorite book. Place emphasis on different words by saying them loudly or quietly.

- Say a funny tongue-twister five times fast and then five times slow, such as, "She sells sea shells by the seashore."

Tool 5-23. Guidelines for Using Webcams During a Virtual Event

When using a webcam during a virtual presentation, meeting, or class, there are three general principles to remember (Figure 5-2).

1. **Place a light source in front of you.** Just like a still photograph, the subject should look into the light for best clarity. This is true for webcams as well. Place a lamp so that the light shines in your face.

2. **Be aware of your background.** It should be a neutral, nondescript environment that does not distract attention. Check to see what's in view of the camera and take action to remove anything that doesn't "fit."

3. **Place the camera at eye level.** Move your webcam so it's at eye level. For most of us, this means elevating your laptop onto a higher surface so that you aren't looking down upon it.

Figure 5-2. Webcam Photos

Improperly Set Up Shot   Properly Set Up Shot

Looking Good on Camera: Tips From a Professional Makeup Artist

Some facilitators and presenters use their webcam for streaming video during the entire session. It's appropriate to do so when the goal is to have a presentation, a webcast, or an online meeting where everyone will be on camera.

Over the years, I've frequently heard people say, "I'm not turning on my webcam because I didn't brush my hair today" or some similar remark. While a facilitator's appearance is not the primary focus of an event, it also shouldn't be a distraction. Facilitators should give at least some thought to how they look. Because many facilitators, myself included, aren't used to applying camera-ready makeup, I reached out to Brett Freedman, a Los Angeles–based makeup artist, for tips. Here is his insightful and helpful response:

"Skin photographs and looks most flattering when matte. This goes for men also. Keep blotting sheets, powder, or mattifier lotion on hand. I suggest Clean & Clear blotting films, MAC Blot Powder, or Benefit Porefessional mattifier.

A lot of women tend to add makeup to the eyes to downplay dark circles. I'd suggest using a good concealer to brighten the under eye. You want just enough eye makeup to give the eyes a crisp, dressed-up look, but not overdone. Laura Mercier makes terrific concealers. Find a shade and formula just for your skin type and coverage.

Avoid too dark or muddy-looking blushes. Choose natural-looking, juicy pinks or peaches that mimic the natural glow of the skin. Avoid blushes with brown or mauve undertones. They may be good in the evening, but they can rob the face of color and look ruddy. I love MAC Mineralize blush in True Romance as a universally flattering blush shade.

Curl lashes. Mascara on uncurled lashes can actually close up the appearance of the eye. I like to curl before mascara and again once it's dry. Be sure the curl on the lashes is just at the lash line, and give a gentle, not full, squeeze. I suggest L'Oréal Voluminous mascara.

Keep brows soft and light. Avoid darkening to a point they compete with the lash line. The lashes should be the boldest thing on the face. Use brow fill-in like watercolors, not a Sharpie. You want to be able to see the brow hairs, not obscure them. This way they frame the eyes and have depth. I suggest Laser Brow pencil from my Brett Brow line."

Summary

Successful virtual classes don't happen by accident. They are a result of careful planning and preparation by virtual facilitators and producers who think ahead. The partnership between these session leaders, and how well they work together, leads to effective online learning programs.

CHAPTER 6

Prepare Participants

Design, check. Delivery, check. Technology, check. You're all set, right? Many training professionals would think so, but you're still missing one key piece of the success puzzle: the participants! Every piece of the puzzle is important, but it's the participants who make the complete picture. The emphasis placed on their preparation can be the difference between effective and noneffective programs.

This chapter puts participants at the forefront of your attention, where they should be when planning virtual training.

Importance of Preparing Participants

Participant preparation needs special focus for several reasons. First, virtual learning is a new experience for many of them. In a traditional environment, participants blocked their calendars, left their workspace, and physically moved themselves to a classroom. They attended a formal training event and then returned to their workspace. While some participants may have found it challenging to maintain focus during class, they were at least in a room with other like-minded learners.

In a virtual training program, we ask participants—in the midst of their workspace and in the middle of their workday—to stop what they're doing, make a mental shift, and focus on learning. We also ask them to concentrate on practicing new skills while they can still see their daily to-do task list on their desk. Distractions abound and entice their attention away from the online program. Even the most disciplined of learners will struggle with this challenging task.

Additionally, virtual training programs compete with other scheduled events on participants' calendars. For most, days are fully scheduled without breaks. Participants "run" from one online meeting to the next, and when "next" is a virtual training event, they may have trouble shifting their participation levels from a passive conference call observer to an active learning participant. Yet that's what an interactive virtual training program asks them to do.

Finally, most employees are being asked to do more and more with less and less. We all are trying to figure out how to do things faster and be more productive. This type of efficiency is a good thing. Yet in stark contrast, the thought of slowing down—as beneficial as it can be—

rarely exists in the modern workplace. So the ideas of pausing to attend training, reflecting on lessons learned, and contributing to personal development can get lost when compared with the seemingly important priority of "getting things done."

Given these factors, it's not surprising that participants have trouble focusing and paying attention in virtual training classes. Therefore, taking extra time to plan for their involvement and set them up for success is a key component of virtual training effectiveness.

How to Prepare Participants

First, everything we have covered so far in this book contributes to the participant experience. Having stakeholder support and buy-in goes a long way toward building a supportive learning culture in the organization. Selecting the right technology creates a simple and easy participant experience. Designing for engagement creates relevant, interactive programs (as opposed to boring, static ones). A dynamic facilitator can capture participant attention and enable learning. Each one of these things is significant and helps set the stage for active participant involvement.

Second, remember that new processes require new thinking. Virtual training is a new way to learn, and therefore, participants need a new mindset. So I recommend borrowing from classic change-management techniques that will help participants adjust to this new way of learning. When things are new, many people struggle to change. A few will embrace it, many will be ambivalent to it, and some may even actively resist it! Anything we can do to assist their embrace of virtual training will be helpful. For example, gain participant support and buy-in by including representatives in initial stakeholder meetings and training rollout. Communicate early and often about virtual training expectations. Prepare learners in advance so that they can be ready. Make extra effort to focus on the participant experience. Share success stories. All of these things will help participants gain a positive mindset about virtual training.

Third, set expectations in advance of every virtual program. More on that in the next section.

Setting Expectations Early

Setting expectations in advance helps people know exactly what to expect when they attend a virtual class. It also helps drive the behaviors—engaged active participants—that you strive for in the virtual classroom.

There are three points when you have a prime opportunity to establish expectations. The first is when participants initially sign up for the program. The program description and all marketing messages should indicate the type of interactive session it will be. The message of interactivity should be reinforced in each reminder message, along with any other pre-class communication. Second, when participants join your virtual event, they should be welcomed into an engaging environment. There should be activities onscreen that draw them in and keep them occupied. It sets the stage for an interactive session if they log in and are immediately expected to participate. Third, at the official start time of the event, participants should be asked to get involved with an activity right away. Chatting with another participant for partner introductions, or responding to a poll question, or even typing on the whiteboard in response to a question are all ways to immediately establish an interactive tone.

To make the most of these three opportunities, plan and carefully script them. This initial investment in advance expectations will result in dividends of participant engagement.

In Action: Partnering Together for Effective Virtual Training at Best Buy

Best Buy's approach to virtual training has created a world-class program that receives accolades and achieves results. Since the program inception, they have taught more than 90,000 associates virtually with offerings that include leadership, product, systems, and services.

Our "extreme attention to details makes it a more valuable experience for participants," says David Beck-O'Sullivan, director of training, learning, and development. "The feedback we're getting from the field is incredible. We see comments such as, 'Wow, I couldn't check my email because I was too busy in the class' and, 'This was way different than I thought it would be; I would have paid money for this.'"

Several factors contribute to Best Buy's success. First, the program design results from collaboration among writers, trainers, and business partners. They conduct a formal intake process, which starts with a brainstorming session, and continue to meet periodically as the program is developed. Part of the design process is detailing the trainers' script word for word. They have learned how to write for virtual programs by reading the scripts out loud to hear how they will actually sound. But don't worry; when the programs come to life, they don't sound scripted. Training manager Jill Jensen says, "By the time I facilitate the class, I've practiced it so much that I'm able to say it in my own words."

Facilitator preparation is another key factor to Best Buy's success. New virtual facilitators go through a rigorous training process to learn Best Buy's methodology. They learn expectations that virtual training should be engaging, entertaining, and valuable. New facilitators shadow experienced ones and spend many hours practicing before they are on their own delivering a class. They even get into details such as listening to one another's recordings to provide feedback on everything from the quality of the microphone to the quality of their voice.

"We want to make sure their experience is the best experience. We're sticklers about preparation to ensure it," says Jensen. "Our virtual training programs are like a morning drive time radio show. It's interesting, engaging, and fun. We keep it fast paced and everyone, including the producer, plays an active role. Our goal is to be super supportive of each other."

Another important detail is the effort put into learner preparation. Best Buy makes use of automated reminders from their learning management system to keep learners informed. The cornerstone to learner preparation is a nine-and-a-half-minute online self-directed program that's a prerequisite to virtual classes. It was created in Storyline with eight tiles and eight short lessons, everything from how to register for programs to how to use the Adobe Connect tools to troubleshooting information. Learners can rewatch each lesson as many times as needed to be prepared for learning.

Finally, Best Buy has tasked one of its team members to be a virtual coordinator, responsible for schedules, reminder emails, and ensuring everyone is prepared. "This has been a very valuable role for us," says Beck-O'Sullivan.

The bottom line? According to Jimmy Bayard, manager of facilitated programs, "Our production value matters. We compete for attention with Facebook, Twitter, phones, and so on. We have to be more interesting than those. We want to focus on the participants . . . we are here to help them learn. We partner together to create a positive learning experience."

Tips, Tools, and Templates

Now that we've established the importance of participant preparation, the rest of this chapter offers the tools, templates, and checklists that will assist you in preparing your participants for a successful learning experience.

Tool 6-1. 5 Ways to Ensure Participants Complete Pre-Session Assignments

Virtual training events rarely happen in a vacuum. They are usually part of a blended training curriculum or a series of virtual events. Therefore, it's common to ask participants to complete an assignment on their own prior to attending class. Unfortunately, many participants don't complete these assignments, for a multitude of reasons. Here are my five favorite ways to get participants to do the pre-work:

1. **Don't call it pre-work.** The term *pre-work* implies that it's not important because it comes before the learning event. Most participants will think that it iss optional information and won't matter if they do it or not. Therefore, assuming it is an important part of the learning journey, use another phrase to describe it. Call it "part 1," "action assignment," or some other term that sounds significant.

2. **Begin a blended curriculum with a live event.** Structure your curriculum in a way that doesn't call for self-directed work prior to the first virtual class. Instead, bring participants together to begin the program and then ask them to complete assignments. This method will establish context for the course work and increase the likelihood of completion.

3. **Add an assessment or test.** By providing an external incentive such as a required test or quiz, participants are much more likely to complete the assignment. This assessment could also be electronically recorded into a learning management system as a prerequisite for the virtual class.

4. **Provide accountability.** Add an element of accountability by having participants report pre-session assignment results to their direct manager or another person to whom they are accountable. For example, ask participants to meet with their manager in advance to set learning goals for the program, and have a communication touch point with managers for check-in.

5. **Include checks and balances in the program design.** One reason many participants don't complete offline assignments is because they won't be asked about it during a training program. Or the facilitator will end up covering the same content as an agenda item, negating any reason for participants to do it in advance. Therefore, include some type of participant report on the assigned content. For example, have a poll question contest on the content to see who can get the most answers correct. Or, using the whiteboard, ask participants to share their biggest insights from the content. Participants who didn't complete it will learn it's an expected part of the learning program.

Tool 6-2. Crafting Your Pre-Session Communication

When writing virtual facilitator guides, I always include a sample pre-session communication message. This message is designed to come from the facilitator, in addition to any automated registration or reminder messages that may come from a learning management system. The following message is one example of that type of communication. A few key points:

- It requests a response, which lets the facilitator know who has read the message.
- It starts a conversation between the facilitator and participant.
- It begins to set the stage for interaction, because it requests activity.

Sample Pre-Session Message From Facilitator

Subject: Welcome From Your Facilitator!

Message:

Hello everyone! I can't wait to meet you online in our upcoming two-part Virtual Facilitation Skills Program!

As you know, we will begin promptly at 11 a.m. Eastern U.S. time (5 p.m. GMT) on Thursday, December 15. We'll meet until 12:30 p.m. ET, and again from 2:30 to 4 p.m. ET that day.

To be prepared, will you please do a few quick things?

- Send me a message with a brief "hello," and let me know what you are most looking forward to about our program. Also, tell me (in just a few words) how you would describe your experience as a participant in virtual events.
- Test your virtual platform connection: {insert test link}.
- Have the attached handout available during our sessions (either print or electronic version).

Also, because our program will be **highly interactive,** please **come planning to participate!** Plan to join from a quiet location that's free from distraction so that you can concentrate online.

You'll need both a computer and a telephone to individually participate, and please don't try to share equipment or space with anyone else. I strongly encourage using a telephone headset so that you can keep your hands free for typing.

You'll join by web using this link: {insert link}, and once you are connected to our virtual classroom, you'll see audio dial-in details onscreen. Please **join the virtual class first** before connecting your audio.

If you have any questions or need assistance, please don't hesitate to contact me.

See you online!

Sending a "Day-of-Event" Message

To continue setting the stage for interactivity and success, I also encourage facilitators to send a "day-of-event" message to participants. This just-in-time reminder helps participants get into the mindset that they have a training event that day. It's nice to have this message waiting in their inbox first thing in the morning. Also, notice that it refers to the requested interaction from the previous reminder, and a copy of the connection link for easy reference.

Subject: Today's the Day! {Name of Program}

Message:

Hi everyone! I can't wait to meet all of you today in our Effective Virtual Training Program!

We'll begin promptly at 11 a.m. ET (5 p.m. GMT), so please plan to **log in** at least five minutes **early** so that you're ready to go.

Here's the connection link for your reference: {insert link}.

You'll see the audio information onscreen as soon as you are connected to the classroom.

Please remember to come planning to participate. Be in a location that's free from distraction so that you can concentrate online. You'll need to individually participate and not try to share a computer or workspace with anyone else.

Finally, a big thank you to everyone who has already responded to my question from the calendar invitation! It's not too late to do so; I'd like to receive a response from each one of you. (The information is below for reference).

Let me know if you have any questions between now and our session start time. See you soon!

Tips for Communicating With Participants

When sending messages to virtual training participants, consider both what you communicate, and how you communicate it.

Content

Make all your communication easy to read with clear and concise text. Take a lesson from marketing professionals who use appealing words and catch phrases to gain attention.

You can do some very simple things to make data easy to read in an email message. For example, if there are strings of numbers that have to be used, such as an event or conference call passcode, then separate numbers into chunks, like "123 45 6789" instead of "123456789."

Also, consider carefully if you will include the session's phone number and passcode along with the web link. In most cases, it isn't necessary because the audio information will be displayed onscreen once a participant joins the virtual classroom. In fact, some platform audio features may not be available if the participants dial in separately, so it's important that they log in to the session first and then follow the audio prompts. By not listing the phone connection, you can force participants to join the session first.

In addition, include class materials, event links, and technical support information in every communication you have with participants. That way, if they have to search for this information, they will easily find it.

Style

Because your participants are likely overloaded with email, it's important to catch their attention with an interesting subject line—something relevant that will entice them to open the message in a timely manner. Once they open the message, you want them to read it, so use color, fonts, and text size to draw their eye to important points. For example, bold the words *join five minutes early* or use a contrast color for the phrase *this will be a hands-on event*.

Remember that many participants read messages on their mobile devices, so consider the implications for format and style. Use large fonts and single-column designs, avoid heavy graphics, and keep the message simple.

Tool 6-3. Helping Participants Prepare

For many participants, it's helpful to have a quick reference guide on how to set up for a virtual event. Here is one that you can share in advance.

Participant Technology Checklist

Technical Needs	❏ Strong (wired) Internet connection ❏ Reliable computer or laptop ❏ Hands-free headset (not a speakerphone) ❏ Sound card for hearing video playback (if used) ❏ Software for virtual classroom platform (if needed)
Other Preparation	❏ Find a quiet space to focus and learn ❏ Set your devices to "do not disturb" mode (hang a sign on your door if needed) ❏ Put away distractions (including "to-do" lists that are in view) ❏ Close out of email and instant messaging programs ❏ Test your connection using the provided link at least 72 hours prior to class start time

Participant Setup Job Aid

Figure 6-1 is another example of a participant setup checklist for a virtual training event. This document is formatted to be a job aid for quick reference, and can be used repeatedly for each class.

Figure 6-1. Sample Setup Guide

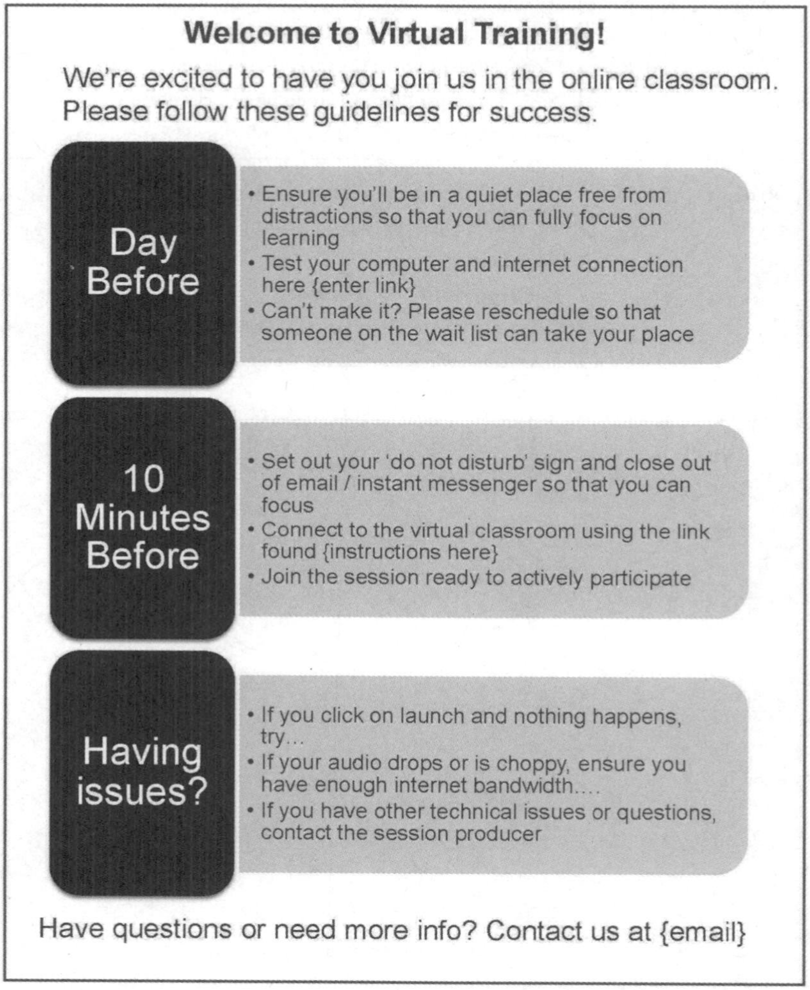

Welcome to Virtual Training!

We're excited to have you join us in the online classroom. Please follow these guidelines for success.

Day Before
- Ensure you'll be in a quiet place free from distractions so that you can fully focus on learning
- Test your computer and internet connection here {enter link}
- Can't make it? Please reschedule so that someone on the wait list can take your place

10 Minutes Before
- Set out your 'do not disturb' sign and close out of email / instant messenger so that you can focus
- Connect to the virtual classroom using the link found {instructions here}
- Join the session ready to actively participate

Having issues?
- If you click on launch and nothing happens, try...
- If your audio drops or is choppy, ensure you have enough internet bandwidth....
- If you have other technical issues or questions, contact the session producer

Have questions or need more info? Contact us at {email}

Tool 6-4. 7 Ways to Help Participants Minimize Distractions

Because paying attention in virtual classes is so difficult for many participants, here is a quick list of tips to share with your facilitators and participants to help eliminate or at least reduce distractions:

1. Invite participants to attend class from an alternative location, such as a nondescript conference room with minimal distractions. By physically moving away from their everyday workspace, participants will eliminate many of their distractions.

2. Ask participants to close out of email, and to raise their hands once they've done it. This in-class activity creates a culture of accountability, and adds peer pressure.

3. Direct participants to put their "do not disturb" notice on instant messaging programs. Invite everyone to do this, and give them a few moments to do so.

4. Include a poll question at the beginning of a class asking people to share if they are willing to stay focused and not get distracted. The poll could be individualized or anonymous; either way, it signifies that distractions should be minimized.

5. Establish ground rules at the beginning of class and ask everyone to commit to following them.

6. Let participants' managers know in advance the time and date of the class, and ask for their support in creating time and space for the employee to learn.

7. Create a strong motivation for participants to stay engaged. For example, invite participants to share in chat the biggest personal benefit to them for actively engaging in the program; that is, how paying full attention will help them in their job role.

Tool 6-5. 3 Ways to Teach Participants the Virtual Platform

Sometimes a reason that participants don't engage is because they are unfamiliar with the virtual classroom platform. Therefore, to eliminate this excuse and give participants a chance to fully engage in the learning, it's important to teach them the platform tools.

There are several ways to help them learn. Here are three of the most common:

1. **Require an introduction to virtual learning prerequisite program.** This 30- to 45-minute live online program spends time going through the major platform tools and how they are used. Its purpose is to set learners up for success whenever they take a virtual class (Tool 6-5).

2. **Hold a mini training session on the tools at the beginning of the event.** By adding this topic to the beginning of every class, it ensures that all learners are on the same page about the content and how to use it for learning (Tool 6-6).

3. **Teach tools in the moment.** This is my preferred way to help participants learn the features. It gives everyone a just-in-time overview of the tool that will be used. This way, I don't have to assume that everyone remembers how to use a tool, and everyone is getting the same instruction (Tool 6-7).

The next three tools are sample agendas and scripts for each of these three methods.

Tool 6-6. Sample Agenda: Introduction to a Virtual Learning Prerequisite Program

This program could be live online or self-directed, although I prefer and recommend live online whenever possible. Invite participants to attend this session as close to their first virtual class as possible. A week in advance is ideal; it's close enough to the event that they won't forget the content, but they'll still have time to adjust their computer or workspace as needed. Also, keep this session as interactive as possible, both to set expectations of participation, and to help everyone learn how to use the tools.

Topic	Content
Start-before-the-start	Invite participants to introduce themselves in chat once they are connected to the session (name, location, role, etc).
Welcome	Brief greeting from facilitator.
Platform experience	Poll question to find out participant experience with the platform. (First time as attendee? Attended before? Used other platforms?)
Introductions	Annotation interactive exercise: Have participants mark their current location on a photo of a map (use either a pointer or marker to note location). Have them raise their hand once they have made their mark.
Benefits and challenges of virtual training	Conduct a dual chat exercise (if your platform allows for multiple chat windows to be open at the same time. Otherwise, make it an annotation interactive exercise using a whiteboard divided in half with a line). Ask participants to type benefits and challenges of virtual training (half of the screen is benefits, other half is challenges). Debrief to discuss points raised, relating them to participants' current experience with virtual training.
Virtual engagement guidelines	Post a list of expected participant engagement guidelines during a virtual class. Ask participants to agree or disagree with the list.
What to expect—content	If participants will attend the same virtual program, share the program outline. Use a poll question to ask for topics of special interest.
What to expect—platform tools	Review any platform tools not yet used during the session, and reinforce the ones already used.
Next Steps	Logistics for next virtual class, along with any assignments to complete between now and then.

Tool 6-7. Sample Agenda Script for Teaching Platform Tools at the Beginning of a Virtual Class

The benefit of beginning a virtual session with an overview of the platform tools is that every attendee will learn how to use them. The drawback is that it could be review for some attendees who already know the platform. It also has the potential to be just a demonstration, which negates the goal of starting with immediate engagement.

To Script or Not to Script?

It should be noted that there is healthy debate among designers over whether facilitator guide notes should be scripted. On the one hand, a scripted guide creates consistency among facilitators because they know exactly what should be said to explain a topic, and what questions will generate the most discussion. On the other, a scripted guide could lead to an unprepared facilitator who simply reads the guide in a monotone voice. Even scripted guides should be used as a "guide" and not a rote memorization activity for delivery.

If you're going to teach the tools at the beginning, make it interactive instead of a passive demonstration. You can use the following facilitator script as a guide.

SAY

Let's begin by introducing ourselves in the chat window. Make sure your chat window says "Send to: Everyone" and type a greeting. Then tell us your name, location, and job role. {Acknowledge responses}

SAY

During our session, we'll be using the status indicator buttons found {location in the platform}. Click once to select it, and click a second time to clear it.

- Raise your hand to ask a question or in response to my questions. For example, raise your hand if you have already had a birthday this calendar year. {Acknowledge all responses.}

- Use the green check for "yes." Use the red x for "no." Click on the green check if you have had a cup of coffee or tea already today; click on the red x if you have not. {Acknowledge all responses.}

SAY

There are other choices as well, such as laughter, applause, and an "away" status. Try choosing one of the other indicators.

SAY

At times during today's session, you'll be asked to type on the whiteboard.

The pointer is the very first tool in the toolbar. Click on it and then click anywhere on the screen. There's your pointer. Now, click somewhere else onscreen and notice how your pointer shows up in that location.

SAY

Next is the marker. Click on it and then start drawing freeform on the whiteboard. You can mark or draw lines; have fun! {Allow a few moments for participants to draw, then erase all annotations.}

SAY

Now, let's try typing. Find the "T" tool—this lets you type text onscreen. Click the *T* and then click anywhere onscreen to start typing. Note that no one else will see what you've typed until you click away from what you typed and somewhere else on the screen.

SAY

You can change your text color, size, and font using the options available. You can also use the eraser to delete anything. Simply select the item and then delete it.

SAY

We'll also use poll questions today, and I'll guide you through those as each one is asked.

ASK

What questions do you have about the platform? Either raise your hand or enter them into chat.

Tool 6-8. Sample Agenda Worksheet for Teaching Tools in the Moment

This is my preferred method for teaching participants how to use a tool. It's just-in-time and only when needed. The facilitator says a few extra words each time a new classroom feature is used, the producer helps everyone use the tools, and participants can engage in the activities.

The best way I know how to show this method is to share a sample design document for the beginning of one of my programs. Notice which platform tools are used and in what order. By intention, they start simple and then increase in difficulty.

Objective	Activity
Start-before-the-start	Warm-up activities to welcome everyone; annotation icebreaker question onscreen to get them chatting, typing, and raising hand.
Welcome	• Brief greeting from facilitator and introductions in chat window • Agenda through poll question (Which of these outcomes most interest you today?)
Recognize benefits of defusing angry customers when providing service	• Raise hand: Ask, who has ever dealt with an angry customer on the telephone? {Acknowledge responses.} • Show slide/whiteboard with sample angry customer statements on it. Say: Review this list and use the marker drawing tool to make a dot next to any of these statements that you have heard. • Ask, what other statements have you heard angry customers say? Please type them either in chat or directly on the whiteboard. • Agree/disagree: Ask, who wants to learn the best ways to respond to these types of statements? (lighthearted question, all should respond "agree") • Transition statement: Let's learn the first technique. . .

Tool 6-9. Options for Distributing Participant Materials

Most virtual classes include participant reference materials that will be used during and after the learning event. Because virtual training participants are remote, they need to somehow receive the materials. Here is a list of distribution methods, along with the pros and cons of each.

Method	Pros	Cons
Mail or ship physical materials	• Materials will be printed to specification • Books and other types of nontraditional materials can be included (product samples, etc.)	• Can be expensive • Must be shipped well in advance of a session
Download from LMS or online repository	• Materials can be easily posted and updated • No printing costs	• Participants have to take initiative to access, download, and print • Participants may need tech support to access or download • Participants take on the cost of printing (paper, ink, etc)
Email to participants in advance	• Registered participants receive materials they need • No extra cost	• Email attachments usually have size limits • Participants have to take initiative to access, download, and print • Sometimes, participants must be on approved sender's lists for email messages to be received
Use platform's file transfer feature	• Shared just-in-time with participants in the session • No extra cost	• Takes time during the program • Participants may not be able to print at that time

Tool 6-10. Connecting to a Virtual Class

When participants get to stay in their workspace for attendance in virtual classes, they could be in almost any location for the event. Share the following tips with them for creating an appropriate learning space for each type of environment.

Tip Sheet: Connecting to a Virtual Class from Various Locations

Location	To Do
Office Cubicles	☐ Post a "do not disturb" sign on your door or cubicle wall. ☐ Use headphones for virtual class audio. ☐ Put away any unnecessary files or papers so that your desk is clear.
Home	☐ Let your family know not to disturb you during class. ☐ Post a sign on your front door asking people not to ring the doorbell. ☐ Have dog or cat treats available to quiet noisy pets. ☐ Check Internet connection speeds to ensure sufficient bandwidth.
Hotel	☐ Ask for a quiet room location, away from the elevator and ice machines. ☐ If using Wi-Fi, select the highest speed available.

Encouraging a Quiet Space for Participants

If participants will be joining a virtual training class from a busy office environment, then I like to share a "do not disturb" sign along with the participant materials. Encourage them to print and hang it on their office door, cubicle wall, or other conspicuous place that everyone will see. It may not eliminate all disruptions, but it will help. Figure 6-2 is a sample of one that can be used.

Figure 6-2. Sample Do Not Disturb Sign

Tips From a Travel Expert: Joining Virtual Events From the Road

Marcey Rader is an internationally known health and productivity coach and the founder of the Work Well. Play More! Institute. She's also the author of *Beyond Travel: A Road Warrior's Survival Guide.* Here's her expert advice on joining virtual events from the road.

- Before logging on, go into your browser settings and clear your history and all temporary files so your operating system will load and play video quicker.

- Streaming and file sharing takes much more speed than regular surfing of the Internet. If you have a poor connection, the live feed will buffer. At a hotel, you are competing with hundreds of other devices that may also be streaming.

- If you can connect using an ethernet cord, you will receive data faster than using Wi-Fi. This will help prevent buffering.

- If there is an option to upgrade to a faster speed, do it. It will be worth the money. This is especially important if you are a facilitator. High speed is relative and doesn't mean it will be as fast as your office or at home. Speed depends on the time of day, what it's being used for, and the service provider.

- If you are a facilitator, log on at least 30 minutes early so you can make sure that you have fast enough speed. You may have to go to another area of the hotel or cozy up to the hotel staff and see if you can spend an hour in an unused meeting room with a separate Internet channel.

- If your face is being seen, prop your computer up or sit low enough that you have it angled appropriately.

- If you have to log on from an airport or coffee shop, remember to mute your line. This is important even if the facilitator mutes everyone because if they are unmuted later for questions, your session participants won't hear the grinding of coffee beans or departure information.

- Always wear a headset, even if you are in your hotel room. You can't control when guests will talk loudly in the hall, a door will slam, or the elevator will ding.

Tool 6-11. Troubleshooting Guide for Participant Connections

If you discover that participants are continually having technical issues when connecting to your virtual classes, use this troubleshooting guide to help pinpoint and solve the issue.

Challenge	Potential Solutions
Poor audio quality	❑ Use a headset to connect. Avoid using speakerphones. ❑ Check to see that enough Internet bandwidth is available. ❑ Use telephone connection instead of VoIP.
Poor visual quality	❑ Check to see that enough Internet bandwidth is available. ❑ Close out of all other applications before joining the event. ❑ Close out of the virtual event and rejoin from a new browser window.
Unable to connect to event	❑ Check to see if they have correct URL. ❑ Check the session password (if there is one). ❑ Download any necessary software. ❑ Run a platform "tech check" (link usually available from supplier).

Tool 6-12. Virtual Class Participant Roster Template

Many learning management systems offer automated reporting on participant registration and attendance. Another simple way to capture attendance is to ask participants to type their names and email addresses into chat or on a whiteboard and then save it. However, if you have to capture participant attendance manually, you can use this template.

	First Name	Last Name	Email	Location	Attended?
	Adam	Smith	asmith@abc.com	East Region	Y
1					
2					
3					
4					
5					
6					
7					
8					
9					
10					
11					
12					
13					
14					
15					

Tool 6-13. Offering Certificates of Completion

If your organization provides certificates for attendance or completion of programs, then this template (Figure 6-3) could be completed and sent electronically to each participant.

Figure 6-3. Sample Certificate of Completion

Alternatively, you could create and send a digital badge (Figure 6-4). Similar to printed paper certificates, digital badges show program completion or achievement. They are often stored online in repositories and displayed virtually.

Figure 6-4. Sample Digital Badge

Summary

The number one reason we conduct virtual training programs is to enable participant learning. Therefore, the learner experience should be at the forefront of everyone's minds when planning programs. Intentional focus on participant preparation is what sets apart great virtual training from average virtual training. The amount of effort will pay off in the long run, in terms of learning and organizational results, which is covered in the next and final chapter, on evaluation.

CHAPTER 7

Evaluate Results

It's easy to say that you want a successful virtual training program. However, it's hard to know what you mean by successful unless you quantify and measure results. What does your organization look for when you say "success"? Are you just checking to see if participants liked the program? Or do you consider it a success when the technology worked as planned and no one got kicked out of the online classroom? Do you look at things like knowledge transfer and on-the-job behavior change? Or something else?

To determine the success of your virtual training programs, you should create an evaluation strategy and measure results. This chapter will help you think through evaluation methods by providing tools, templates, and checklists that help you measure the success of your virtual training programs.

Why Evaluation?

Evaluation is the process of determining the effectiveness of a training program. It involves collecting, reviewing, and analyzing data that point to a program's success (or lack thereof). Evaluation data could come from surveys, interviews, focus groups, observations, business reports, or other sources. By gathering and interpreting these data, you measure the impact of the training program. And then by communicating these results, you can show the positive effect the program had on participants and on the organization. Without measuring results, you will only be guessing at the program's effectiveness and whether or not it was worth it.

For example, I recently helped an organization create a virtual training program on problem solving. The program's goal was to equip associates with problem-solving skills so that they could efficiently respond to issues that were affecting organizational performance. Once the program was launched, how would it be considered a success? We could ask the facilitator what they think of the program and ask participants if they like the program. We could ask business unit leaders if they have seen a decrease in performance problems. We could also wait until a few months after the program finishes and then ask participants if they have used any of the skills they learned to solve problems. Or we could use a combination of the above to measure success. All of them provide measurements, and all could be used to define varying stages of success.

Evaluation Basics

While there are several ways to evaluate the effectiveness of training programs, the most common method is Donald L. Kirkpatrick's four levels of evaluation. Although his book *Evaluating Training Programs* was published in 1994, he originally outlined the four levels in a series of articles published in 1956. Organizations use the model to tell if lessons learned in training programs are applied on the job and contributing to business results.

How to Use the Kirkpatrick Four Levels

In Kirkpatrick's evaluation model, Level 1 measures participant reaction to the program. Finding out what they thought about the learning experience, the facilitator, the materials, and the topic provides insight into the program's effectiveness. Level 2 measures participant learning. This step seeks to discover what they learned about the program topic. Level 3 checks to see if participants are applying the new knowledge and skills back on the job. This measure typically takes place at least 30 days after the training program ends. Finally, Level 4 examines the program's impact on organizational business results. For example, did the customer service training affect customer satisfaction scores? Did the management development program result in reduced employee turnover? Did the database training lead to reduced data entry errors and more efficient productivity?

The next step beyond the four levels is to measure return on investment (ROI). While it's not part of the Kirkpatrick model, ROI is commonly referred to as "Level 5" evaluation. Jack and Patti Phillips have written extensively about how to measure ROI in training programs, and their model is considered the industry's gold standard. In its simplest form, ROI measures the monetary benefit of a program divided by the program costs. If the program cost $10,000 to create and implement, and a $20,000 sale was made as a result of it, then the program realized a 100 percent return on investment.

How to Use the ROI Methodology

In any organization, owners, shareholders, and leaders want to spend money wisely. And when money is spent, they want to ensure it will bring a beneficial return to the organization. This idea is true for training programs as well. When an organization devotes money to designing, developing, and delivering a training program, most leaders will think it's important to gain a return on that investment. Sometimes this return is intangible, in the form of increased employee loyalty or improved communication among teammates.

A typical ROI measurement takes the program costs, divides them by benefits realized, and multiplies them by 100 to arrive at a percentage. Jack Phillips's ROI model for training programs is the most common ROI model in use. In his words, ROI "shows the monetary benefit of the impact measures compared with the cost of the program. This value is typically stated in terms of either a benefit-cost ratio, the ROI as a percentage, or the payback period. This level of measurement requires two important steps: First, the impact data (Level 4) must be converted to monetary values, and then the cost of the program must be captured" (Biech 2014).

The ROI calculation is as follows:

$$\frac{\text{Net Program Benefits}}{\text{Program Costs}} \times 100 = \text{ROI}$$

Because all program costs must be in the calculation, when calculating ROI for virtual training programs, be sure to include all technology costs, including teleconferencing fees, supplier support fees, and any host licenses or other platform expenses, as well as a prorated amount to cover participant salaries and benefits.

In Action: Calculating ROI at Banner Health

Becoming a leader at Banner Health meant automatic enrollment in the Leader Academy, a one-week in-person classroom experience. The week included learning from senior leaders who traveled from the corporate offices to deliver content. It was a high-energy, fun event, which unfortunately had a high price tag.

When the organization needed to cut expenses across the board, every group was asked to contribute ideas on how to save money. So Mike Abrams, senior director of talent optimization, proposed a redesign of the Leader Academy. He put together a team of stakeholders representing different business units from across the organization, and began the transformation.

Mike's team determined that converting the Leader Academy to an all-virtual program would save the organization $300,000 a year. To arrive at this number, he totaled up the "hard" expenses, including travel, printing, shipping, and catering, and then subtracted the expenses incurred for virtual delivery. The new program eliminated travel, shipping, and catering. It moved the printing expenses from corporate to a shared responsibility with the learners, who were sent a set of job aids and reference cards to print as desired.

The training team also considered the "soft" expenses of the original program and realized benefits of the revised program, and discovered gains in this area as well. In the original Leader Academy, senior leaders who taught modules had to step away from their essential roles for extended periods of time to facilitate. For the revised virtual Leader Academy, subject matter experts were recruited to facilitate the content, which also became a development opportunity for them.

Beyond the initial conversion and cost savings realized, Mike's team was able to start offering even more programs than they had been able to in the original structure. The training team had more time to develop and deliver efficient, targeted classes.

The overall gains seen by Banner Health made this program conversion from classroom to virtual a worthwhile investment with lasting returns.

Creating an Evaluation Strategy

A recent ATD research study on evaluating learning found that while 88 percent of organizations evaluate some learning programs at Level 1, and 83 percent evaluate some learning programs at Level 2, only 60 percent measure some programs at Level 3, and 35 percent measure organizational impact (Level 4) of some programs (ATD 2016). The numbers are smaller when considering only technology-based programs. In that case, organizations in the study reported evaluating 58 percent of programs at Level 1, 51 percent at Level 2, 18 percent at Level 3, and 13 percent at Level 4 (ATD 2016). These fascinating numbers give insight into organizational behavior around the evaluation of training programs.

Most organizations seem to care about what participants think (Level 1), and provide some type of survey to collect these data. However, while organizations may want to know if their programs are adding value to the business, very few programs are actually measured this way. It could be due to lack of resources, lack of time, lack of knowledge in how to capture these results, or many other reasons. In my experience, it's often because evaluation decisions are either left up to chance, or left until after the program has rolled out, and by then it's often too late. Or, it's because training programs are implemented without taking time to do any analysis, which in turn makes it hard to measure results. It also could be because they lack the knowledge and skills to do it.

When creating an evaluation strategy, it should start at the very beginning, when you are first considering the training program. The end results should be considered from the beginning. Ideally, the evaluation process begins when a business problem is discovered and analyzed, and the training program is one of the recommended solutions. If the process gets started this way, then the results can be measured by going back to see if the business problem was solved.

For example, let's say your customer database has considerable data entry errors, and it's discovered that these errors stem from employees not knowing how to use the system. You therefore design and implement a data entry training program, and then point to the reduced number of data entry errors as the measure of your program's success. Most everyone would agree that this example would be a picture of success.

Most everyone would also agree that many training programs are not that simplistic or straightforward when it comes to evaluation. Perhaps it's a new hire orientation program, the safety and compliance programs offered on an annual basis, product training for the sales team, or some other interpersonal skills program that you intuitively know employees need. How do you go about creating an evaluation strategy for those programs? How will you know if they are a success?

Ideally, all training programs are designed, developed, and implemented because their goal is to help participants do their jobs better. And whatever tells you how they can "do their jobs better" is one of the measurements to use for program success. You discover this information in the initial analysis phase of program design.

For instance, the goal of new hire orientation is to acclimate new hires and enable them to become productive employees faster. Safety and compliance programs keep employees safe.

Product training gives the sales team the information they need to sell. And so on. In each of these examples, there is some tangible measure of success that could be used to determine results. And this measure is determined in the analysis phase, when the program is first formed.

The evolution of an evaluation strategy continues with the design phase. Designers should create the solution to meet business needs. They write learning objectives that align with the participant's performance measures. They develop the structure and sequence of a program so that it leads to learning transfer. They provide enough time for participants to practice the new skills. These design decisions may not seem like they have much to do with an evaluation strategy, but if a program isn't designed with results in mind, it will be difficult, if not impossible, to measure those results.

Next, the evaluation strategy continues to take hold in the development phase. As the program is developed, real-world, relevant practice opportunities should be built into it. Formative evaluation opportunities, such as gathering incremental feedback from stakeholders, should be incorporated.

Finally, the evaluation strategy should be firmly in the minds of facilitators and others who are implementing the program. They should be aware of the learning objectives, follow the design as structured, provide ample opportunities for practice, and engage participants in the learning as often as possible. Facilitators should be observing and providing performance feedback as participants practice their new knowledge and skills. And because facilitators are usually the ones who distribute and gather participant feedback, they should ensure that this important step occurs.

Evaluation for Virtual Training

So far, everything I've said about evaluation would be true for any training program. What, then, makes evaluation different in a virtual training program? Admittedly, not much. Evaluation is evaluation regardless of the program, just like training is training regardless of the modality.

Except for the important fact that virtual training platforms often provide built-in tools that can easily capture evaluation data. And virtual programs by nature have a dispersed audience; therefore, using electronic methods to collect evaluation data is prevalent and preferred.

Capturing evaluation data using virtual platforms makes use of its technology. Most virtual classroom software programs include polling, and many include a quiz or test feature. These tools can be used for both Level 1 (reaction) and Level 2 (learning) evaluation data. In addition, many platforms allow website sharing, which easily connects participants to an external survey host. If your organization uses a survey tool, then that tool can quickly be incorporated into a virtual program (Figure 7-1). Finally, as discussed in chapter 3, many virtual platforms integrate with the LMS, which can capture poll, quiz, and survey results for reporting.

Figure 7-1. Adobe Connect Web Links Pod

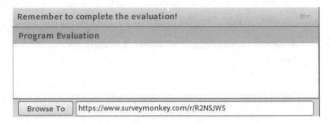

In Action: Evaluating Virtual Training at Coventry Health Care

In April 2012, the learning and performance team at Coventry Health Care chartered a metrics committee. The committee was tasked with measuring performance improvement and organizational impact of all training programs (Level 3 and Level 4 of the Kirkpatrick model). They embraced this ambitious goal by setting out to learn all they could about measurement and evaluation. The result is a robust measurement process that quantifies the impact of virtual training.

The team uses a blended approach to measure these results, with a variety of data collection methods. For example, they use electronic survey tools to measure participant reaction and test knowledge. They also look for post-program behavior change of participants by collecting hard data from their business systems. They use the Phillips ROI method to isolate effects of the training on organizational impact. And they have implemented many methods from the Six Disciplines approach to learning transfer.

According to Jon Hurtado, senior learning consultant, "What sets us up for success are the strong learning objectives that come from a robust needs assessment. These learning objectives have a prominent role in every training program. Facilitators make frequent references to them, not just at the beginning, but throughout. Since learners are exposed to the objectives multiple times, they are able to see the progress they're making toward the outcomes. Therefore, when we go to measure post-program results, we are able to use those objectives and refer back to them. Learners are so familiar with them that they know what we're measuring. It helps us determine results."

Tips, Tools, and Templates

Your virtual training programs may be wildly, off-the-charts successful. But if no one knows about it, then the results may all be for naught. If you take the time to measure the results of virtual training, then communicate those results to stakeholders. The tips, tools, checklists, and templates that follow will help you do so.

Tool 7-1. Host a Lessons-Learned Meeting

After a virtual training program has been designed, it's always a good idea to pilot it before a full implementation. During this pilot phase, the designer should gather feedback from all stakeholders involved, including facilitators, producers, and pilot participants. This lessons-learned meeting agenda is similar to the one in chapter 6, but it involves more stakeholders. The meeting contributes to the "formative" evaluation, which means the evaluation data collected will help you "form" the final program.

Lessons Learned Meeting Agenda

Here are some discussion points to include in the lessons-learned meeting:

- What worked well overall?

- What should be changed for next time?

- How did the actual activity timing compare with the expected timing?

- What, if any, changes should be made to the facilitator and producer guide?

- What, if any, changes should be made to the slides and other visual aids?

- What, if any, changes should be made to the participant materials?

- Were the participants engaged throughout the program? If not, what reasons contributed to that?

- Was there enough variety in the activities to keep participant attention?

- What else should be noted about the program?

Post-Pilot Action Tracker (Formative Evaluation)

During the post-pilot (after-action) review meeting, use this form to track updates and actions to take.

	Item	Responsibility to Do	Comments	Estimated Timing	Complete By:
1	Fix typos and page formatting issues	CLH	See notes in workbook	2 editing hours	July 1
2					
3					
4					
5					
6					
7					
8					
9					
10					

Tool 7-2. Reference Chart: Levels of Evaluation

The most common framework for evaluating training programs is the Kirkpatrick model, usually referred to as the four levels of evaluation. Here is a quick reference chart for each of the levels.

Level	Description	Question Answered
1	Reaction	What was the participants' reaction to the program? Did they like it? Did they appreciate the facilitator? Did they think the program materials were useful? Would they recommend it?
2	Learning	Did the participants achieve the program's learning objectives? Do they know more about the topic than they did before the program?
3	Behavior	Are participants using the new knowledge and skills back on the job? How has their behavior changed? Which job productivity measures have improved?
4	Results	What business results have been realized? Has the organization or business unit achieved its operational goal?

Tool 7-3. Tips on What to Evaluate in Virtual Training Programs

When creating an evaluation strategy, organizations often struggle to determine what data to collect, and whether it's worth investing resources in the evaluation. For guidance, I asked Ken Phillips, a Chicago-based expert in training evaluation, to share his wisdom. Here are his tips:

First, all virtual training programs should be evaluated at least through Level 1. Also, at a minimum, data should be collected on three topics:

1. **The platform:** How well did it work, how easy was it to sign in and navigate, how clear was the audio, how did any polls that were used work, and so forth.

2. **The facilitator:** How knowledgeable was the facilitator about the topic, how well did the facilitator keep everyone engaged, how well did the facilitator respond to participant questions, and so forth.

3. **The program:** How relevant was the program, how much did participants know about the topic before attending the program and how much do they know after attending, and so forth.

Next, to determine the number of additional levels of evaluation to include beyond Level 1, four factors should be considered:

1. How strategically important is the program?

2. How costly is the program?

3. How many participants are going to attend the program?

4. What does the business executive stakeholder expect or want?

For programs where one or more of these factors is present, additional levels of evaluation should be considered.

Tool 7-4. Evaluation Strategy Planner Worksheet

With the advice on the previous pages, this worksheet will help you plan a training program evaluation strategy. You may notice some similarities with the goal-planning worksheet found in chapter 1 (Tool 1-2) because there is overlap between goal planning and evaluation mapping. Both items seek results.

Name of the Virtual Training Program:

What's the big goal for this program? What specifically do you hope to accomplish? What do the stakeholders want to accomplish?

What do participants need to do as a result of this training program?

- ❐ Be more knowledgeable about the topic
- ❐ Behave differently
- ❐ Take action on something
- ❐ Other:

How will the organization or business unit change or improve as a result?

What are the program's measurable learning objectives?

Rate the following factors on a scale of 1-5. (The higher the total, the more important it will be to have an evaluation strategy.)

	Low 1	2	3	4	High 5
How strategically important is the program?	❏	❏	❏	❏	❏
How costly is the program?	❏	❏	❏	❏	❏
How many participants will ultimately attend the program?	❏	❏	❏	❏	❏
Totals for each column					

What type of evaluation does the business executive stakeholder expect or want?

Given all of the above, what level of evaluation will you strive for?
- ❏ Level 1
- ❏ Level 2
- ❏ Level 3
- ❏ Level 4

What data collection measures could you capture for each level selected above?

Level	Description	Data to Collect
1	Reaction	
2	Learning	
3	Behavior	
4	Results	

What else should you note about the evaluation strategy for this program?

Tool 7-5. Creating Level 1 Surveys

When I'm delivering virtual train-the-trainer and train-the-designer programs, this is the simple Level 1 survey that I typically share with participants' post-program. It's short and easy for participants to complete, and it gives me just enough feedback to make program improvements.

Level 1 Survey Template 1

1. Would you recommend this program to others who are interested in virtual facilitation (or virtual training design)?

   ❐ Yes
   ❐ No

2. What are the reasons for your response?

3. What other comments or thoughts do you have about the program?

Level 1 Survey Template 2

Here is a more detailed version of a participant reaction survey.

Please provide feedback on your virtual training experience by rating your agreement with each statement below.

	Strongly Disagree	Disagree	Neither Agree nor Disagree	Agree	Strongly Agree
The program objectives were clear.					
The program met its stated objectives.					
The activities and exercises helped me learn the program material.					
The program materials (slides, handouts, and other visuals) were useful during the program.					
It was easy to use the virtual classroom tools (chat, polls, status indicators).					
The facilitator was knowledgeable about the subject matter.					
The facilitator promoted participant discussion and engagement.					
I chose to actively participate in the program (typing in chat, responding to polls, engaging in the activities).					
This program provided information that I need to know and will use in my current role.					
I'd recommend this program to others.					

What was the most valuable part of the program?

What program improvements would you suggest?

What other program comments do you have?

Tool 7-6. Other Ways to Collect Level 1 Feedback in a Virtual Class

A virtual facilitator can collect participant feedback using the tools in the virtual platform. Here are several ways that could be accomplished.

Plus/Minus Whiteboard

This technique allows you to ask about what worked well in this program (plus) and what participants would change (minus). Participants can individually write their responses on the board (Figure 7-2).

Figure 7-2. Plus/Minus Whiteboard

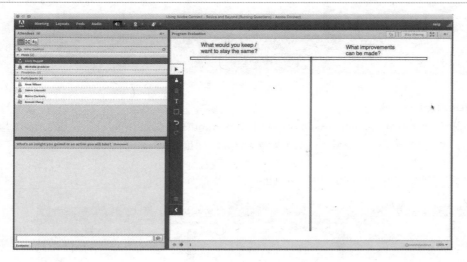

Chat Discussion

This technique allows the facilitator to post questions and capture participants' written responses. Multiple questions can be answered by either asking them one at a time or opening multiple chat windows (Figure 7-3).

Figure 7-3. Using Chat for Program Evaluation

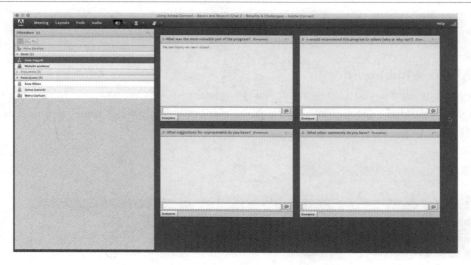

Poll Questions

This technique allows participants to respond anonymously to multiple-choice questions. Some platforms also allow for polls with short text answers (Figure 7-4).

Figure 7-4. Using Polls for Program Evaluation

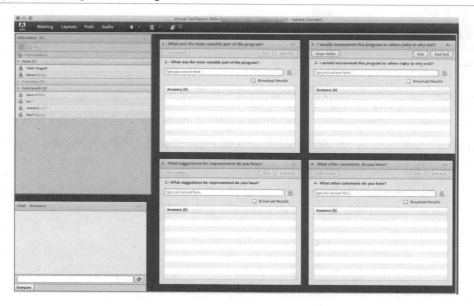

Tool 7-7. Guidelines for Writing Level 2 Evaluations

According to Ken Phillips, a noted expert in learning evaluation strategy, most Level 2 evaluations use multiple-choice questions to test for knowledge. The best multiple-choice questions are intentionally written to match up with the program objectives. Use Ken's guidelines to write them effectively:

- Be sure there is only one correct answer.

- Test for application, not just knowledge or recall.

- Keep response options equivalent in length and writing style.

- Don't reveal the correct answer in the questions.

- Ensure that all response options are plausible.

- Write questions in the same way the material was taught.

- Include the central idea and most of phrasing in the stem.

- Write the stem as a question—responses can finish the question, but don't use a fill-in-the-blank format.

- Use at least four response options for each item.

- Avoid use of "all of the above" and "none of the above."

- Spread correct answers across A-D.

- Eliminate excessive verbiage or irrelevant information from the stem.

- When possible, present the response options in some logical order, such as chronological, most to least, or alphabetical.

- Make all response options mutually exclusive.

Tool 7-8. Steps to Create Level 2 Evaluation Test Questions

Knowledge transfer is typically measured during a virtual training program by tests, quizzes, or skills demonstrations. If you will be using tests or knowledge checks, then you will most likely be writing multiple-choice questions.

Here are Ken Phillips' tips for creating Level 2 multiple-choice test questions that measure job application and not mere recall. The value of these types of questions is that they not only test for whether a participant learned something, but also whether the participant knows how to apply it back on the job.

1. Select a training learning objective and think about what learners need to know and do to meet the objective.

2. Think of real-life situations that reflect actual application of the program content covered by the objective. Make notes describing each of the situations.

3. Chose one of the situations and write the stem (the question or problem) in one to three sentences. Some possible item shells when writing application test items are:
   - "What is the most (least) effective method for . . .?"
   - "What is better (or worse) . . .?"
   - "What would happen if . . .?"
   - "What is the most (least) critical step in the process?"
   - "What is the most appropriate solution to this problem?"
   - "What is the next step to solve this problem?"
   - "What is the nature of this problem?"
   - "What is needed to solve this problem?"

4. Identify plausible distracters—think of things someone might say or do who thought they knew the content of the learning objective, but really didn't understand it.

Tool 7-9. Tips for Collecting Level 3 Evaluation Data

Level 3 evaluation data—behavior change—is typically collected at least 30 days after a program has been completed. This time lapse usually gives enough space for participants to apply what they have learned, and a gives a chance for results to be realized.

When gathering these data, you could survey the participants to find out if they are using the content learned. You could also survey the participants' direct managers to inquire about on-the-job behavior change. Neither of those are perfect methods because they involve opinion instead of solely relying on facts. However, these behavioral surveys are the simplest and easiest, especially with a remote workforce.

If you have the time and resources, you could observe the participants in action using the learned skills. This would mean either checking their performance records, or watching them complete a task. For example, if you wanted to see if employees were following the new entry procedures they learned in last month's safety training program, you could have a team of raters stand watch at the factory entrance to see who follows the new entry procedure. Or, if you wanted to see if managers were writing performance expectations using SMART goals as they learned in their management development program, you could arrange with HR to confidentially review team performance goal submissions by manager. This type of work observation can get you the highest-quality data; however, it may not be feasible given the resource requirements.

If you will be creating a behavioral survey to collect Level 3 data, remember the following tips, adapted from Ken Phillips' expert advice:

- Double check that the program learning objectives are in alignment with the desired on-the-job behavior change.

- Write statements that describe the types of behaviors someone might engage in who attended the program, learned the content, and was applying what had been learned back on the job.

- Focus only on observable, measurable behaviors, not thoughts or motives—that is, "Participant responded to the customer complaint using an approved defusing technique" versus "Participant considers the customer complaint before responding with an approved defusing technique." .

- Limit each statement to a single behavioral description—that is, "Participant responded to the customer complaint using an approved defusing technique" versus "Participant responded to the customer complaint using approved defusing technique and then offered the customer a discount on their next purchase."

- The survey should be two-thirds positive (behaviors the person does) and one-third negative (behaviors the person does not do). Write positive statements for all behavior items, and then identify a third of them to rewrite in reverse.
  - Positive example: "Participant responds to customer complaint using approved defusing techniques."
  - Negative example: "Participant does not respond to customer complaints using approved defusing techniques."

- If using a rating scale, use measures of frequency (how often)(never/always) instead of agreement (agree/disagree) or effectiveness (very effective/not effective).

- If using a rating scale, put lowest number on the left and highest number on the right ("1-5,"not "5-1").

Tool 7-10. Creating a Level 3 Evaluation Data Report

Several years ago, I facilitated a leadership development program. I was interested to hear from participants on how they were applying skills they learned. About 45 days after the program ended, I sent a simple survey with three questions, asking them to respond to at least one question. The anecdotal results were so powerful that I shared them with the organization's executive leadership. Figure 7-5 is the sample report that I shared.

The three I questions asked were:

1. What is at least one thing you have learned as a result of this program?
2. What is one thing you have done differently as a result of this program?
3. In what situation have you applied something you learned from this program? Describe the situation and what you did.

Figure 7-5. Sample Level 3 Report

Participants in the leadership program were asked to answer one of the following questions. Here are several responses that show business impact:

1. **What is at least one thing you have learned as a result of this program?**
2. **What is one thing you have done differently as a result of this program?**
3. **In what situation have you applied something learned from this program? Describe the situation and what you did.**

"I've looked at performance appraisals in a different manner. I'm able to prioritize job responsibilities based on the employees' job descriptions and relate them to company goals."

"When giving a person a new assignment, I make sure they understand the task, commit to it, get their feedback, and have set deadlines to follow up."

"I'm on a big job that's in process of closing down. It's the time when you start losing people but still need to have stuff done. I worked with a young project engineer [and] encouraged him to take action. As a result it has alleviated many problems on the project that would otherwise typically occur."

"I've learned the importance of providing constructive feedback based upon facts."

"I had several midyear reviews to do. Learning how to help my employees prioritize most of their tasks has been very helpful."

"I've become a more positive communicator and listener. I've been able to focus on the solution instead of focusing on the person or trying to fix the person."

"I've worked with our warehouse manager, who had multiple tasks and responsibilities. His priorities were different than the company's priorities. I scheduled a meeting with him. The results were great. We've met deadlines on time as a result."

"On my project, I had some employees who had to deal with rough spots. There were many changing priorities from the owner. I learned how to explain the changes to them [and] why the changes were happening, and help them work through the issues."

Tool 7-11. Collecting Level 4 Evaluation Data

To measure the organizational impact of your virtual training program on the organization, you have to know what data are important to the organization. What key indicators are measured? What statistics are reported? What numbers do organizational leaders focus on when reporting to owners or other stakeholders? These data points should also be the measures of success for your training programs. This chart shows an adapted summary of most common measures that organizations use for Level 4 evaluation data.

Measure	Percentage
Business leader perception of impact	74%
Customer satisfaction	60%
Employee satisfaction/engagement	44%
Actual business outcomes	44%
Learner perception of impact	39%
Productivity indicators	37%
Turnover and promotions	33%

Source: ATD (2016).

If the organization is tracking these types of data, it should be fairly easy to capture the numbers. What's notoriously difficult, however, is being able to say that these numbers changed as a result of your training program. You could use a control group, trend line analysis, or other estimates to determine the training's impact. Nevertheless, most Level 4 results are reported with caveats and exceptions to explain the other potential influences.

Summary

Although evaluating results is the last full chapter in this book, it's not the last step of a virtual training program. Create an evaluation strategy at the start of your program. Begin thinking about how you will measure success, gain buy-in and agreement from your stakeholders, and start collecting data from the program inception. That way, when it's time to evaluate success, you won't be stuck wondering what to measure or how to measure it. Planning ahead will save you time and will help you show the positive impact of your virtual training programs.

Epilogue

In 2013's *The Virtual Training Guidebook,* I predicted three trends for the future of virtual training: MOOCs (or massive open online courses), mobile, and microbursts. Four years is practically a lifetime in technology, so it's time to revisit each trend to see how it has evolved and its influence on virtual training. In addition, two more significant trends have recently appeared, so I've added them to the list for consideration.

In short, the five trends to watch are:

- MOOCs (and virtual learning environments, or VLEs)
- mobile
- microbursts
- modern
- metrics.

Let's take a closer look at each one.

MOOCs

"What's interesting to me, and the reason I believe MOOCs and VLEs are an important future trend to consider, is that they can place a single virtual training class into a larger context."

—*The Virtual Training Guidebook,* p. 183

The *New York Times* declared 2012 the "Year of the MOOC" because hundreds of thousands of learners were attending these courses (Pappano 2012). They seemed to be a promising path forward for corporate education. The reason I thought they would have a future impact on virtual training is the inclusion of synchronous, live online events in between the self-paced activities. I grouped MOOCs with VLEs as examples of blended learning curriculums. And I advised instructional designers to be aware of the trend toward creating blended programs.

Today, MOOCs are almost exclusively associated with asynchronous, self-paced learning events as opposed to live online classes, and therefore no longer a relevant influence on virtual training.

However, blended programs, including virtual learning environments, are thriving. One report pegs blended learning as 86 percent of all learning provided, and predicts that number will continue to rise (Mimeo 2016). Because virtual training comprises up to 58 percent of blended learning events, it's time to take notice (Chapman 2013).

If it's not already happening in your organization, it likely will soon. Instructional designers will be asked to design virtual training events in the context of blended learning curriculums. Facilitators will be asked to assist participants in their learning journey both inside and outside the virtual classroom. And administrators will manage many separate components of a cohesive program.

Also, because the term *blended learning* is the more relevant phrase to describe training programs with multiple components in one curriculum, I'll stop referring to this trend as MOOCs and instead call it "multidimensional."

Mobile

"As devices get more sophisticated, and apps are developed for live online training, we are certain to see an increased usage of mobile devices for virtual training."

—*The Virtual Training Guidebook,* p. 184

There's no question that mobile devices have permeated our daily lives. We use our devices for work, for communication, for fun, and for just about every other use imaginable. So it's no surprise to see that mobile devices continue to be a trend with significant impact on virtual training.

There are two items of special interest about the impact of mobile devices on virtual training. First, participants are more likely to use their devices to connect to virtual training events. They access the online classroom through the device's browser, or the link prompts them to join through the platform's app.

Yet that's the biggest challenge about this trend, as noted earlier in the book. There is a disconnect between the desktop browser version of most virtual classroom platforms and the corresponding mobile app. While there has been vast improvement in recent years, many virtual classroom apps simply do not support the robust features available on the desktop.

Eventually—I hope—platform suppliers will be able to make fully functional apps. Or, they'll create a new type of platform that's device agnostic. In the meantime, training professionals can be ready for this eventual shift by staying abreast of changes in mobile technology and scanning for new platforms that come to market.

Second, even if participants connect to an event through their computer, their mobile device is probably not far from their hand. It's estimated that people check their smartphones up to nine times per hour (Aamoth 2013). If they are participating in a virtual event and their mobile device is nearby, they will be faced with extra temptation to multitask. Therefore, each one of the techniques learned earlier in this book about designing for engagement are especially important to incorporate into your virtual training.

Microbursts

"Virtual training is ideally poised to meet the trend of shorter and faster training classes. In many ways it is already filling that need due to its typical 60- to 90-minute length. However, in the future, I believe we will see even shorter classes, or what I would consider to be a 'microburst' of learning."

—The Virtual Training Guidebook, p. 185

The trend toward shorter, more concise training programs began years ago, and continues today. It's not just programs that are getting shorter, but seemingly everything. We text instead of email, for example, and use emoticons or emojis instead of words.

In 2010, the average virtual training class was 90 minutes long. Today the average is closer to 60 minutes, based upon my experience and the shared experience of my colleagues. Virtual programs that last longer than 60 or 90 minutes typically include breaks, just like a traditional in-person class.

The idea of shorter virtual training programs is a good thing. Shorter bursts of learning translate to better on-the-job results (Kapp et al. 2015). And shorter programs also help avoid cognitive overload for participants.

Therefore, virtual training designers should create short online segments whenever possible, interspersing them with hands-on practice assignments. When converting classes from in-person to online, designers should figure out how to chunk program content into microsized pieces that can be easily consumed.

Modern

"Put quite simply, the modern learner is any corporate employee today. The modern learner's attributes, expectations, and demands have shifted from those of corporate learners even just five years ago, not to mention previous decades. And corporate learning has had to catch up."

—Intrepid Learning (n.d.)

The term *modern learner* was introduced in 2008. It reached heightened popularity in 2014, when a set of curated statistics was published in an online infographic that went viral (Tauber and Johnson 2014). That fascinating capsule of facts summarized information about trends and pressures in the 21st-century workplace. To illustrate how common this descriptive phrase has become since then, a quick web search for "modern learner" yields more than 16 million results.

This book has described the reality of modern virtual learners: they are distracted, overwhelmed, and overloaded. They are connected online and use multiple devices with ease. They are on the go and can work from remote locations. They have high expectations for technology, and want a seamless online experience. They also want to collaborate with other participants, believing it's an essential part of the learning experience. Modern learners aren't limited to a certain age or demographic—they can be found anywhere in the workforce or around the globe.

There are several ways to accommodate this trend of virtual training participants as modern learners. First and most important, design virtual training that allows for social connections. Create opportunities for participants to interact with one another throughout an event. Place them into pairs or breakouts, and do team activities. Let them collectively solve problems that lead to learning outcomes.

Second, use all available platform tools to invite interactivity throughout the program. Purposefully design it so that learners are engaged from the moment they log in. Again, use the tips and techniques in this book to help.

Metrics

"By analyzing complex data sets across functional silos, organizations are gaining insights to help catalyze change, improve access to experts, speed onboarding, retain talent, and identify root causes for complicated issues. It improves the learning environment, and even the Learning & Development organization itself."

—*Gail Dutton* (2014)

Measurement of training program impact is not a new concept. However, what's happening with measurement and evaluation is enough to take notice and include it in the list of trends.

First, as noted in chapter 7, 60 percent of organizations measure some training programs for on-the-job learning transfer (Level 3; ATD 2016a). This is notable because just seven years prior, in a similar study, only 23 percent of organizations reported measuring Level 3 results (ASTD 2009). This increased emphasis on evaluating learner success provides several opportunities for the virtual training team. With positive evaluation data, you can demonstrate value, justify investments, and improve program quality.

In addition to increased interest in measurement, more organizations and training departments are making use of data analytics. Information of all kinds can be collected, sorted, and analyzed to uncover problems and find solutions. For virtual training, you could examine everything from registration trends to best pre-session communication methods and even to learner engagement in the classroom. For learning transfer, you could measure the business impact of those who attended the programs. Of course, the results will only be as good as the data collected, and your ability to comb through the large data sets to find patterns.

To effectively glean relevant information from data captured, virtual training professionals should find out what data are collected at the organizational level. They should partner with others in the organization who are also searching for information. And they should increase their analytical skills to manipulate and export relevant information from large data sets.

Summary

To stay updated on these trends, do three things. Keep an eye on the news headlines for trend updates. Keep your ears open for feedback from your own learners. And keep your hands on the steering wheel as you drive learning solutions in your organization. These three actions will keep your virtual training heading in the right direction.

References

Aamoth, D. 2013. "Study Says We Unlock Our Phones a Lot Each Day." *Time,* October 8. http://techland.time.com/2013/10/08/study-says-we-unlock-our-phones-a-lot-each-day.

ASTD (American Society for Training & Development). 2009. *The Value of Evaluation: Making Training Evaluations More Effective.* Alexandria, VA: ASTD Press.

ATD (Association for Talent Development). 2016a. *Evaluating Learning: Getting to Measurements That Matter.* Alexandria, VA: ATD Press.

———. 2016b. *State of the Industry.* Alexandria, VA: ATD Press.

———. 2017. *Virtual Classrooms Now: Using Technology to Reach Today's Workforces.* Alexandria, VA: ATD Press.

Biech, E., ed. 2014. *ASTD Handbook: The Definitive Reference for Training and Development,* 2nd edition. Alexandria, VA: ASTD Press.

Chapman, B. 2013. *Large Scale, Blended Learning Development: Benchmark.* Chapman Alliance LLC.

Cisco. 2016. "10th Annual Cisco Visual Networking Index (VNI) Mobile Forecast Projects 70 Percent of Global Population Will Be Mobile Users." Cisco, February 3. https://newsroom .cisco.com/press-release-content?type=webcontent&articleId=1741352&utm_source=cisco .com&utm_campaign=Release_1741352&utm_medium=RSS.

Clark, R.C., and A. Kwinn. 2007. *The New Virtual Classroom.* San Francisco: Pfeiffer.

Dirksen, J. 2012. *Design for How People Learn.* Berkeley, CA: New Riders.

Dutton, G. 2014. "What's the Big Deal About Big Data?" *Training,* May 13. https://trainingmag .com/trgmag-article/what%E2%80%99s-big-deal-about-big-data.

Huggett, C. 2010. *Virtual Training Basics.* Alexandria, VA: ASTD Press.

———. 2013. *The Virtual Training Guidebook.* Alexandria, VA: ASTD Press.

Huggett, C., and W. Gates Corbett. 2008. "Simple, Effective Online Training." *Infoline.* Alexandria, VA: ASTD Press.

Intrepid Learning. n.d. "The Modern Learner." Intrepid Learning. www.intrepidlearning.com /modern-learner.

Kapp, F., A. Proske, S. Narciss, and H. Körndle. 2015. "Distributing vs. Blocking Learning Questions in a Web-Based Learning Environment." *Journal of Educational Computing Research* 51(4): 397-416.

Kapp, K.M., and R.A. Defelice. 2009. "Time to Develop One Hour of Training." Learning Circuits, August 31. www.td.org/Publications/Newsletters/Learning-Circuits/Learning-Circuits-Archives /2009/08/Time-to-Develop-One-Hour-of-Training.

King, S. 2014. "The #1 Enemy of Online Conferences—Poor Audio Quality." ReadyTalk Blog, May 20. www.readytalk.com/blog/scott-king/the-1-enemy-of-online-conferences-poor -audio-quality.

Kirkpatrick, D.L. 1956. "How to Start an Objective Evaluation of Your Training Program." *Journal of the American Society of Training Directors,* May-June.

Kirkpatrick, D.L., and J.D. Kirkpatrick. 2006. *Evaluating Training Programs: The Four Levels,* 3rd edition. San Francisco: Berrett-Koehler.

Kirkpatrick, J.D., and W.K. Kirkpatrick. 2016. *Kirkpatrick's Four Levels of Training Evaluation.* Alexandria, VA: ATD Press.

LaBorie, K., and T. Stone. 2015. *Interact and Engage! 50+ Activities for Virtual Training, Meetings, and Webinars.* Alexandria, VA: ATD Press.

Medina, J. 2008. *Brain Rules.* Seattle: Pear Press.

Mimeo. 2016. *The State of Learning and Development 2016.* New York: Mimeo.

Pappano, L. 2012. "The Year of the MOOC." *The New York Times,* November 2. www.nytimes .com/2012/11/04/education/edlife/massive-open-online-courses-are-multiplying-at-a -rapid-pace.html.

Pew Research Center. 2017. "Mobile Fact Sheet." Pew Research Center, January 12. www .pewinternet.org/fact-sheet/mobile.

Pike, R.W. 2002. *Creative Training Technique Handbook,* 3rd edition. Amherst, MA: HRD Press.

———. 2011. "Creative Training Techniques for Webinars: Seven Ways to Add Impact and Wow—NOW!" Session presented at ASTD TechKnowledge 2011, San Jose, CA, February 2011.

Shank, P. 2010. *Getting Started With E-Learning: Synchronous E-Learning.* Santa Rosa, CA: The eLearning Guild.

Strayer, D.L., and J.M. Watson. 2012. "Supertaskers and the Multitasking Brain." *Scientific American Mind* 21(1): 22.

Tauber, T., and D. Johnson. 2014. "Meet the Modern Learner (Infographic)." Bersin by Deloitte, November 26. www.bersin.com/Practice/Detail.aspx?id=18071.

Tracey, R. 2008. "Connectivism and the Modern Learner." E-Learning Provocateur, December 28. https://ryan2point0.wordpress.com/2008/12/28/connectivism-and-the-modern-learner.

List of Tools

Chapter 1

Tool 1-1. A Thought Starter: Is Virtual Training the Right Solution?

Tool 1-2. Organizational Analysis Tool

Tool 1-3. Goal-Planning Worksheet

Tool 1-4. Brainstorming for Success Worksheet

Tool 1-5. Benefits Checklist: Which Will You Realize?

Tool 1-6. Virtual Training Definition Brainstorm

Tool 1-7. Virtual Training Definition Documents

Tool 1-8. Stakeholder Identification Checklist

Tool 1-9. Virtual Training Budget Template

Tool 1-10. Benefit-Cost Analysis Worksheet

Tool 1-11. Building the Business Case

Tool 1-12. Strategy Planning Meeting

Tool 1-13. Virtual Training Project Team Charter and Strategy Template

Tool 1-14. RACI Model

Chapter 2

Tool 2-1. Technology Planning Worksheet

Tool 2-2. Building a Relationship With IT

Tool 2-3. Common Virtual Classroom Platform Tools

Tool 2-4. Comparison Between Platform Tools for Meetings, Training, and Webcasts

Tool 2-5. Questions to Ask During a Virtual Training Platform Demo

Tool 2-6. Comparing Hosted Versus On-Site Technology Solutions

Tool 2-7. Checklist for Selecting a Platform

Tool 2-8. Audio Options Worksheet

Tool 2-9. Sample RFP Template

Tool 2-10. Technology Requirement for Facilitators and Producers Checklist

Tool 2-11. Technology Requirements for Participants Checklist

Chapter 3

Tool 3-1. Template for the 3-Step Design Process

Tool 3-2. Best Practices for Converting In-Person Classes to Online Classes

Tool 3-3. The ADDIE Model and This Book

Tool 3-4. Sample Design Standards Checklist for Virtual Training

Tool 3-5. Checklist for Upskilling Traditional Instructional Designers in Virtual Training

Tool 3-6. Virtual Instructional Designer Job Description

Tool 3-7. Components to Design and Develop for a Virtual Training Initiative

Tool 3-8. 5 Tips for Partnering With SMEs on Virtual Class Design

Tool 3-9. Guidelines for Shaping a Blended Learning Curriculum

Tool 3-10. Sample Template for Blended Learning Design

Tool 3-11. Sample Design Document

Tool 3-12. Design Document Template

Tool 3-13. Putting Together the Facilitator Guide

Tool 3-14. Tips for Creating Participant Materials

Tool 3-15. Designing for Webcasts

Tool 3-16. Designing for Hybrid Programs

Tool 3-17. Sample Session Planner for Hybrid Audience Program

Chapter 4

Tool 4-1. 5 Reasons to Develop Preprogram Content

Tool 4-2. Start-Before-the-Start Activity Planner

Tool 4-3. Planning an Open Activity

Tool 4-4. Outline: Welcome Message From a Senior Leader

Tool 4-5. Developing Activities for Virtual Training Classes

Tool 4-6. 5 Energizer Activity Ideas

Tool 4-7. 10 Tips for Incorporating Media into Virtual Training Design

Tool 4-8. 5 Closing Activity Ideas

Tool 4-9. Worksheet: Questions to Ask When Creating an Activity

Tool 4-10. Guidelines for Sequencing Activities in a Virtual Class

Tool 4-11. Guidelines for Creating Slides for Virtual Training

Tool 4-12. 7 Tips for Making Online Lectures, Presentations, and Webcasts Interactive

Tool 4-13. Developing Activities for a Global Audience

Chapter 5

Tool 5-1. Reference Chart for Virtual Training Roles and Responsibilities

Tool 5-2. Comparison Between Traditional Classroom Facilitation and Virtual Facilitation

Tool 5-3. List of Skills Needed for Virtual Facilitation

Tool 5-4. Virtual Facilitator Job Description

Tool 5-5. List of Skills Needed for Virtual Producing

Tool 5-6. Interview Questions for Potential Virtual Facilitators and Producers

Tool 5-7. Ideas for Producer Resources

Tool 5-8. Technology Checklist for Virtual Facilitators

Tool 5-9. Tips for Learning Technology

Tool 5-10. Setting Up a Virtual Facilitation Workspace

Tool 5-11. The Extra-Prepared Virtual Facilitator and Producer Checklist

Tool 5-12. Checklist for Facilitator-Producer Pre-Session Rehearsal

Tool 5-13. Checklist for Facilitator-Producer Post-Session Debrief

Tool 5-14. Get to Know Your Audience Worksheet

Tool 5-15. Day-of-Event Planning Checklist for Virtual Facilitators and Producers

Tool 5-16. Facilitation Techniques for Engaging Virtual Participants

Tool 5-17. Virtual Delivery Tips for Success: A Quick Reference Guide for Facilitators

Tool 5-18. Facilitator Considerations for Culturally Diverse Audiences

Tool 5-19. Developing Virtual Facilitators and Producers

Tool 5-20. A Facilitator's Guide to Responding to the Unexpected

Tool 5-21. The Skill of Multitasking

Tool 5-22. Vocal Warm-Up Exercises for Virtual Facilitators

Tool 5-23. Guidelines for Using Webcams During a Virtual Event

Chapter 6

Tool 6-1. 5 Ways to Ensure Participants Complete Pre-Session Assignments

Tool 6-2. Crafting Your Pre-Session Communication

Tool 6-3. Helping Participants Prepare

Tool 6-4. 7 Ways to Help Participants Minimize Distractions

Tool 6-5. 3 Ways to Teach Participants the Virtual Platform

Tool 6-6. Sample Agenda: Introduction to Virtual Learning Prerequisite Program

Tool 6-7. Sample Agenda Script for Teaching Platform Tools at the Beginning of a Virtual Class

Tool 6-8. Sample Agenda Worksheet for Teaching Tools in the Moment

Tool 6-9. Options for Distributing Participant Materials

Tool 6-10. Connecting to a Virtual Class

Tool 6-11. Troubleshooting Guide for Participant Connections

Tool 6-12. Virtual Class Participant Roster Template

Tool 6-13. Offering Certificates of Completion

Chapter 7

Tool 7-1. Host a Lessons-Learned Meeting

Tool 7-2. Reference Chart: Levels of Evaluation

Tool 7-3. Tips on What to Evaluate in Virtual Training Programs

Tool 7-4. Evaluation Strategy Planner Worksheet

Tool 7-5. Creating Level 1 Surveys

Tool 7-6. Other Ways to Collect Level 1 Feedback in a Virtual Class

Tool 7-7. Guidelines for Writing Level 2 Evaluations

Tool 7-8. Steps to Create Level 2 Evaluation Test Questions

Tool 7-9. Tips for Collecting Level 3 Evaluation Data

Tool 7-10. Creating a Level 3 Evaluation Data Report

Tool 7-11. Collecting Level 4 Evaluation Data

Recommended Resources

I encourage you to continue learning about designing, delivering, and implementing effective virtual training. If you are interested in diving deeper into these topics, then here are a few resources from my own bookshelf that I recommend.

Publications

Biech, E, ed. 2014. *ASTD Handbook: The Definitive Reference for Training & Development*, 2nd edition. Alexandria, VA: ASTD Press.

———. 2015. *101 More Ways to Make Training Active.* Hoboken, NJ: John Wiley & Sons.

———. 2016. *The Art and Science of Training.* Alexandria, VA: ATD Press.

Bozarth, J. 2013. *Better Than Bullet Points: Creating Engaging E-Learning With PowerPoint,* 2nd edition. San Francisco: Wiley; Alexandria, VA: ASTD Press.

Brandon, B., ed. 2008. *144 Tips on Synchronous Learning Strategy + Research.* Santa Rosa, CA: The eLearning Guild.

———. 2008. *The eLearning Guild's Handbook on Synchronous E-Learning.* Santa Rosa, CA: The eLearning Guild.

Carnes, B. 2012. *Making E-Learning Stick: Techniques for Easy and Effective Transfer of Technology-Supported Training.* Alexandria, VA: ASTD Press.

Carliner, S. 2015. *Training Design Basics,* 2nd edition. Alexandria, VA: ATD Press.

Christopher, D. 2011. "Facilitating in the Global Virtual Classroom." *Infoline.* Alexandria, VA: ASTD Press.

———. 2014. *The Successful Virtual Classroom: How to Design and Facilitate Interactive and Engaging Live Online Learning.* New York: AMACOM.

Clark, R.C., and A. Kwinn. 2007. *The New Virtual Classroom.* San Francisco: Pfeiffer.

Clark, R.C., and R.E. Mayer. 2016. *E-Learning and the Science of Instruction: Proven Guidelines for Consumers and Designers of Multimedia Learning,* 4th edition. Hoboken, NJ: John Wiley & Sons.

Clay, C. 2012. *Great Webinars: How to Create Interactive Learning That Is Captivating, Informative and Fun.* San Francisco: Pfeiffer.

Courville, R. 2009. *The Virtual Presenter's Handbook.* www.eventbuilder.rocks.

Dirksen, J. 2015. *Design for How People Learn,* 2nd edition. Berkeley, CA: New Riders.

Gates Corbett, W., and C. Huggett. 2009. "Designing for the Virtual Classroom." *Infoline.* Alexandria, VA: ASTD Press.

Halls, J. 2014. "Memory and Cognition in Learning." *Infoline.* Alexandria, VA: ASTD Press.

Hodell, C. 2016. *ISD From the Ground Up: A No-Nonsense Approach to Instructional Design,* 4th edition. Alexandria, VA: ATD Press.

Hofmann, J. 2004. *Live and Online!: Tips, Techniques, and Ready-to-Use Activities for the Virtual Classroom.* San Francisco: Pfeiffer.

———. 2004. *The Synchronous Trainer's Survival Guide: Facilitating Successful Live and Online Courses, Meetings, and Events.* San Francisco: Pfeiffer.

Hofmann, J., and N. Miner. 2009. *Tailored Learning: Designing the Blend That Fits.* Alexandria, VA: ASTD Press.

Hubbard, R. 2013. *The Really Useful eLearning Instruction Manual: Your Toolkit for Putting eLearning Into Practice.* San Francisco: Wiley.

Huggett, C. 2010. *Virtual Training Basics.* Alexandria, VA: ASTD Press.

———. 2013. *The Virtual Training Guidebook: How to Design, Deliver and Implement Live Online Learning.* Alexandria, VA: ASTD Press.

Huggett, C., and W. Gates Corbett. 2008. "Simple, Effective Online Training." *Infoline.* Alexandria, VA: ASTD Press.

Kirkpatrick, D.L., and J.D. Kirkpatrick. 2006. *Evaluating Training Programs: The Four Levels,* 3rd edition. San Francisco: Berrett-Koehler.

Koegel, T.J. 2010. *The Exceptional Presenter Goes Virtual.* Austin, TX: Greenleaf Press.

Laborie, K., and T. Stone. 2015. *Interact and Engage!: 50+ Activities for Virtual Training, Meetings, and Webinars.* Alexandria, VA: ATD Press.

McClay, R., and L. Irwin. 2008. *The Essential Guide to Training Global Audiences: Your Planning Resource of Useful Tips and Techniques.* San Francisco: Pfeiffer.

Murdoch, M., and T. Muller. 2013. *The Webinar Manifesto: Never Design, Deliver, or Sell Lousy Webinars Again.* New York: RosettaBooks.

Phillips, J.J., and P.P. Phillips. 2005. *Return on Investment (ROI) Basics.* Alexandria, VA: ASTD Press.

———. 2007. *Show Me the Money.* San Francisco: Berrett-Koehler.

Phillips, P.P., ed. 2010. *ASTD Handbook of Measuring and Evaluating Training.* Alexandria, VA: ASTD Press.

Pike, R.W. 2002. *Creative Training Techniques Handbook,* 3rd edition. Amherst, MA: HRD Press.

Pike Pluth, B. 2010. *Webinars With WOW Factor: Tips, Tricks and Interactive Activities for Virtual Training.* Minneapolis, MN: Pluth Consulting.

———. 2016. *Creative Training: A Train-the-Trainer Field Guide*. Minneapolis, MN: Creative Training Productions.

Reynolds, G. *Presentation Zen: Simple Ideas on Presentation Design and Delivery*, 2nd edition. Berkeley, CA: New Riders.

Russell, L. 2007. *10 Steps to Successful Project Management*. Alexandria, VA: ASTD Press.

Scannell, M., M. Abrams, and M. Mulvihill. 2012. *Big Book of Virtual Team Building Games: Quick, Effective Activities to Build Communication, Trust, and Collaboration From Anywhere*. New York: McGraw-Hill.

Steed, C. 2011. *Facilitating Live Online Learning*. Engaged Online Learning.

Shank, P. 2010. *Getting Started With Synchronous e-Learning*. Santa Rosa, CA: The eLearning Guild.

———. 2011. *The Online Learning Idea Book: Proven Ways to Enhance Technology-Based and Blended Learning, Volume Two*. San Francisco: Pfeiffer.

Smith, D. 2016. "6 Steps to Moving Your Training Online." *TD at Work*. Alexandria, VA: ATD Press.

Turmel, W. 2011. *10 Steps to Successful Virtual Presentations*. Alexandria, VA: ASTD Press.

Udell, C. 2012. *Learning Everywhere: How Mobile Content Strategies Are Transforming Training*. Nashville, TN: Rockbench Publishing; Alexandria, VA: ASTD Press.

Virtual Classroom Software Suppliers

Here are a few examples of common virtual classroom software platforms. Please note that this is not an exhaustive list.

Platform	Website
Adobe Connect	www.adobe.com/products/adobeconnect
Blackboard Collaborate	www.blackboard.com/platforms/collaborate/overview.aspx
Cisco WebEx Training Center	www.webex.com/products/elearning-and-online-training.html
GoToTraining	www.gototraining.com
Jigsaw	http://jigsawme.com
Saba Classroom	www.saba.com/us/lms/virtual-classroom
Zoom	https://zoom.us

Trademark Attributions

Acknowledgments

A special thanks to the many business and training professionals who shared their experience, advice, and stories: Andre Gratton, Brett Freedman, Cindy Keegan, David Beck-O'Sullivan, Dan Nugent, Jack Benedict, Jessica Pyle, Jill Jensen, Jimmy Bayard, Jon Hurtado, Julie Rimkus, Kassy LaBorie, Katie Stroud, Ken Phillips, Lee Slimm, Marcey Rader, Mark Aronson, Michael Merritt, Mike Abrams, Stacy Lindenberg, and Wendy Gates Corbett, along with a few who chose to remain anonymous (you know who you are!). I appreciate each one of them for their willingness to offer their wisdom and lessons learned. Their contributions have greatly enriched this book. Thank you.

I'm also extremely grateful for several individuals who reviewed early versions of the manuscript, including Betsey Upchurch, Kassy LaBorie, Keri DeDeo, and Wendy Gates Corbett. Special thanks also goes to Sherri Stotler for her incredible research and organizational skills. All of their insights were invaluable and made this book much better than it would have been otherwise.

Thank you also to Justin Brusino, Kathryn Stafford, and Caroline Coppel at ATD Press for their enormous patience during the lengthy book-writing process. Their encouragement and advice carried this book through from concept to completion.

Finally, I dedicate this book to Bobby and Jonathan. It was because of their love and support that this book was finished.

Cindy Huggett
Psalm 115:1
June 2017

About the Author

Cindy Huggett, CPLP, is an independent consultant, professional speaker, instructional designer, classroom facilitator, and author who specializes in workplace training and development. With more than 25 years of experience, she has successfully designed curriculums, facilitated classes, and led training rollouts in almost every industry and every size organization. Cindy partners with her clients to help them transition from the face-to-face to the virtual classroom, and works with them to design online and blended learning solutions.

Cindy is the author of three books on virtual training: *Virtual Training Tools and Templates* (2017), *The Virtual Training Guidebook* (2013), and *Virtual Training Basics* (2010). She co-authored two *Infoline* issues, "Simple, Effective Online Learning" (2008) and "Designing for the Virtual Classroom" (2009). She's also contributed to several compilations, including the *ASTD Handbook: The Definitive Reference for Training & Development* and *101 Ways to Make Learning Active Beyond the Classroom,* and written several articles for *TD* magazine.

Cindy holds a master's degree in public and international affairs from the University of Pittsburgh, and a bachelor's degree from James Madison University. She is also a past member of the ATD National Board of Directors and was one of the first to earn the Certified Professional in Learning and Performance (CPLP) designation.

You can find Cindy sharing training tips on Twitter as @cindyhugg, or through her website, www.cindyhuggett.com.

Index

In this index, *f* denotes figure and *t* denotes table.

A

Abrams, Mike, 185
accountability, 111, 163
activities
  about, 93
  advice about, 96–97, 96*t*
  closing, 111, 112*f*
  design process and, 63
  developing, 107
  energizer, 108
  global audience, 119–120
  interactivity, 94–96, 118
  media, incorporating, 109–110, 110*f*
  opening, 104–105
  preprogram content, reasons to develop, 98–99
  questions to ask when creating, 113
  sequencing, 114–115
  slide creation guidelines, 116–117, 117*f*
  standards, 69
  start-before-the-start, 100–103, 101*f*, 103*f*
  tips, tools, templates, 97–120
  welcome message from senior leader, 106
ADDIE model, 68
Adobe Connect, 39, 39*f*, 45*f*, 188*f*
agendas
  lessons-learned meetings, 189–190
  platform tool training, 171–174
  strategy planning meetings, 29–32
  virtual learning prerequisite program, 171
  webcasts, 85–86
annotate and draw tool, 49, 50, 107
application sharing, 49, 50
Aronson, Mark, 67, 127
art gallery review, 111
assessments, 154, 163
assignments, pre-session, 163
Association for Talent Development (ATD), 2, 186
audience. *See* participants
audio, 40, 43–44, 55, 134

B

badges, digital, 181, 181*f*
Banner Health, 185
Bayard, Jimmy, 162

Beck-O'Sullivan, David, 161, 162
behavioral surveys, 201–202
Benedict, Jack, 9
benefit-cost analysis worksheet, 24–25
benefits checklist, 16
Best Buy, 161–162
big-picture questionnaires, 12–13
blended learning
  about, 42
  assignments, pre-session, 163
  curriculum guidelines, 74–76
  design template, 77, 77*f*
  learning management system and, 74
body language, 146
brain teasers, 108
brainstorming, 15, 17
breakouts, 49, 50, 107
budget, 23, 88
business case, building, 26–28, 47
buy-in from stakeholders, 8–9

C

certificates of completion, 181, 181*f*
chair yoga pose, 108
chat, 49, 50, 107, 197, 198*f*
checklists
  benefits, 16
  components, 72
  day-of-event planning, 145
  debrief, post-session, 142
  design standards, 69
  facilitators and producers, 137–140
  multitasking, 154
  platform selection, 54
  rehearsal, pre-session, 141
  stakeholder identification, 21–22
  technology for facilitators and producers, 58, 134
  technology for participants, 59, 167
  technology skills, 135
Choice Hotels, 91
Clark, Ruth Colvin, 95
closing activities, 111, 112*f*
collaboration, 47–48, 73, 161
communication, 47, 73, 119, 164–166

community, creating, 98, 146
completion, certificates of, 181, 181*f*
computers, 138
conference calling, 43, 55
connecting to virtual class, 176–179, 177*f*
content, designing. *See* design
converting in-person classes to online classes, 65–67, 65*f*
coordinators, 127, 162. *See also* facilitators and producers
Coventry Health Care, 67, 127, 188
creativity challenge (activity), 108
culturally diverse audiences, 119–120, 149

D
day-of-event message to participants, 165
day-of-event planning checklist, 145
debrief checklist, post-session, 142
delivery success tips, 148
design
    about, 61
    ADDIE model, 68
    blended learning, 74–77, 77*f*
    components, 72
    converting in-person classes to online classes, 65–67, 65*f*
    design document, sample, 78–79
    design document template, 80
    design process template, 64
    evaluation strategy and, 187
    facilitator guide, 81–82, 82*f*
    hybrid programs, 87–91
    initial step, 61–62
    instructional designer job description, 71
    instructional designers, upskilling, 70
    participant materials creation tips, 83–84
    process, 62–63
    standards checklist, 69
    subject matter experts, partnering with, 73
    tips, tools, and templates, 63–91
    webcasts, 85–86
design documents, 78–80
Design for How People Learn (Dirksen), 76
digital badges, 181, 181*f*
Dirksen, Julie, 76
disengaged attendees, 96*f*
distractions, minimizing, 169
"do not disturb" signs, 177, 177*f*
document sharing, 49
Dutton, Gail, 210

E
energizer activity ideas, 108
engagement, 96*f*, 128, 146–147
English as a second language, 119, 120, 149
evaluation
    benefits of, 183
    formative, 190
    Kirkpatrick model overview, 184, 191
    lessons-learned meetings, 189–190
    Level 1, 184, 186, 191, 195–198, 197*f*, 198*f*
    Level 2, 184, 186, 191, 199–200

Level 3, 184, 186, 191, 201–203, 203*f*, 210
    Level 4, 184, 186, 191, 204
    objects of, 192
    return on investment (ROI) methodology, 184–185
    strategy for, 186–187, 193–194
    tips, tools, and templates, 188–204
    trends, 210
    for virtual training, 187–188, 188*f*
examples, selecting, 120, 147
expectations, setting, 98, 146, 160–161

F
facilitation skills, 129
facilitator and producer guides, 72, 81–82, 82*f*
facilitators and producers
    about, 123–124
    advice from, 143
    checklist, 137–140
    culturally diverse audiences and, 149
    day-of-event planning checklist, 145
    debrief checklist, post-session, 142
    developing, 150–151
    engagement techniques, 146–147
    evaluating, 192
    evaluation strategy, 187
    facilitation skills, 129
    interview questions for potential, 132
    job description, 130
    multitasking, 153–155
    observation forms, 150–151
    participants, getting to know, 144
    producer resources, 133
    producing skills, 131
    rehearsal checklist, pre-session, 141
    roles and responsibilities, 90, 127
    selecting, 125
    success tips, 148
    technology checklist, 58, 134
    technology skills, learning, 135
    terminology, 124–125
    tips, tools, and templates, 126–158
    traditional classroom *versus* virtual facilitation, 128
    two session leaders, benefits of, 124
    unexpected, responding to the, 152
    upskilling, 126
    vocal warm-up exercises, 156
    webcam use guidelines, 157–158, 157*f*
    workspace, setting up, 136, 136*f*
facilities, outsourced, 88
file and material distribution tool, 49, 50, 107
flow, 63
formative evaluation, 190
4 Ts, 74–75
Freedman, Brett, 158

G
getting ready for virtual training
    about, 6–8
    benefit-cost analysis worksheet, 24–25
    benefits checklist, 16

brainstorming worksheet, 15
budget template, 23
business case, building, 26–28, 47
buy-in from stakeholders, 8–9
goal-planning worksheet, 14
implementation, 5–6
organizational analysis tool, 12–13
project team charter and strategy template, 33–34
RACI model, 35
stakeholder identification checklist, 21–22
strategic plan, 9
strategy planning meeting, 29–32
tips, tools, and templates, 10–35
virtual training, appropriateness of, 11
virtual training definition brainstorm, 17
virtual training definition documents, 18–20
global audiences, 119–120, 149
goals, 6, 14
graphics, 72, 120
Gratton, Andre, 91

H

hardware, 38–41, 39f, 134
HDR (company), 45
headsets, 40
home, connecting from, 176
hosts. *See* facilitators and producers
hotels, connecting from, 176, 178
Hurtado, Jon, 188
hybrid programs, 87–90, 91

I

icebreakers, 100–101
implementation, 5–6
In Action feature
    Banner Health, 185
    Best Buy, 161–162
    Choice Hotels, 91
    Coventry Health Care, 67, 127, 188
    HDR, 45
    Mars University, 126
    Volvo Trucks, 9
information technology department, 47–48
insights, sharing, 111, 112f
instructional designers, 70–71
instructors. *See* facilitators and producers
integrated conference calling, 43, 55
Interact and Engage! (LaBorie and Stone), 96, 96f
interactivity, 65, 94–96, 118
Internet bandwidth, 25, 40, 44–45, 45f
Internet connection, 134, 137
interview questions for potential virtual facilitators and
    producers, 132
IT department, 47–48

J

Jensen, Jill, 161
job descriptions, 71, 130

K

Keegan, Cindy, 28
King, Scott, 40
Kirkpatrick, Donald L., 184
Kirkpatrick model overview, 184, 191
Kwinn, Ann, 95

L

LaBorie, Kassy, 96–97, 96f
Leader Academy, 185
learners. *See* participants
learning consultants, 127. *See also* facilitators and producers
learning coordinators, 127. *See also* facilitators and producers
learning environment, 149
learning management system (LMS), 41, 42, 74
learning objectives, 74, 76
lessons-learned meetings, 189–190
Level 1 evaluation
    about, 184, 191
    chat discussion, 197, 198f
    plus/minus whiteboards, 197, 197f
    poll questions, 198, 198f
    surveys, 195–196
    use of, 186
Level 2 evaluation
    about, 184, 191
    test questions, 200
    use of, 186
    writing, 199
Level 3 evaluation
    about, 184, 191
    behavioral surveys, 201–202
    data, collecting, 201–202
    data reports, 203, 203f
    use of, 186, 210
Level 4 evaluation
    about, 184, 191
    data, collecting, 204
    use of, 186
light source, 157
Lindenberg, Stacy, 42
LMS (learning management system), 41, 42, 74

M

makeup tips, 158
Mars University, 126
massive open online courses (MOOCs), 207–208
materials. *See* participant materials
media, 72, 109–110, 110f
meetings, 29–32, 50, 189–190
Merritt, Michael, 45
metrics, 210. *See also* evaluation
microbursts, 209
mini training session at beginning of class, 172–173
mobile devices, 38–40, 39f, 208
moderators. *See* facilitators and producers
modern learners, 209–210
MOOCs (massive open online courses), 207–208
multitasking, 147, 153–155

N

names, scenario character, 120
National Transportation Safety Board, 28
New Virtual Classroom, The (Clark and Kwinn), 95
nonverbal body language, 146
note to self (activity), 111

O

objectives, learning, 74, 76
observation forms, 150–151
office cubicles, connecting from, 176
online portals, 42
openers, topic-connecting, 100–101, 101*f*
opening activity, planning, 104–105
organizational analysis tool, 12–13
outlines, 66, 66*f,* 106
outsourced facilities, 88

P

participant materials
    checklist, 72
    creating, 83–84
    design standards and, 69
    distributing, 49, 50, 107, 175
    for global audience, 120
participant preparation. *See also* participants
    assignments, pre-session, 163
    certificates of completion, 181, 181*f*
    communication, pre-session, 164–166
    connecting to virtual class, 176–179, 177*f*
    distractions, minimizing, 169
    expectations, setting, 160–161
    helping participants prepare, 167–168, 168*f*
    importance of, 159–160
    participant material distribution, 49, 50, 107, 175
    participant roster template, 180
    platform, teaching to participants, 170–174
    process, 160–161
    tips, tools, and templates, 162–181
participants. *See also* participant preparation
    backgrounds, 75
    checklist, 140
    converting in-person classes to online classes, 65
    counts of, 65
    culturally diverse, 119–120, 149
    day-of-event message to, 165
    engaging, 96*f,* 128, 146–147
    English as a second language, 119, 120, 149
    getting to know, 144
    hybrid program design, 88
    late, 100
    modern, 209–210
    platforms/platform tools, teaching, 100, 170–174
    roster template, 180
    setup guide for, 168, 168*f*
    success, setting up for, 99
    technology checklist, 59, 167
partnering, 47–48, 73, 161
perceptions about virtual training, 119

Phillips, Jack, 184–185
Phillips, Ken, 192, 199, 200, 201–202
Phillips, Patti, 184
photo puzzles, 108
platforms and platform tools
    about, 41, 42
    activities, 100, 107
    comparison of, 50
    demos, 51–52
    description and uses, 49
    engagement and, 147
    evaluating, 192
    evaluation and, 187, 188*f*
    interactivity, 95–96
    participants, teaching to, 100, 170–174
    selection checklist, 54
    start-before-the-start activity, 100
    teaching to participants, 100, 170–174
plus/minus whiteboards, 197, 197*f*
polls, 49, 50, 107, 198, 198*f*
portals, online, 42
post-pilot action tracker, 190
post-session debrief checklist, 142
practice, 155
preprogram content, 98–99
pre-session assignments, 163
pre-session communication, 164–166
pre-session rehearsal checklist, 141
producer resources, 133
producers. *See* facilitators and producers
producing skills, 131
project team charter and strategy template, 33–34
Pyle, Jessica, 126

Q

questionnaires, big-picture, 12–13

R

RACI model, 35
Rader, Marcey, 178
raise hand tool, 49, 50, 107
rapport, building, 98, 146
red light, yellow light, green light (activity), 111
referenc   e charts
    evaluation levels, 191
    participant technology checklist, 167
    roles and responsibilities, 127
    virtual delivery tips for success, 148
rehearsal checklist, pre-session, 141
remote interaction managers. *See* facilitators and producers
request for proposal (RFP) template, 56–57
results, evaluating. *See* evaluation
return on investment (ROI) methodology, 184–185
roles and responsibilities, 89, 90, 127

S

scenario character names, 120
scripts, 172–173
self-assessment, 154

senior leader, welcome message from, 106
sequencing activities, 114–115
setup guide for participants, 168, 168f
slides, 69, 72, 116–117, 117f
Slimm, Lee, 143
SMEs (subject matter experts), 73
software, 41–42, 134, 137, 155
stakeholders, 8–9, 21–22
stand-alone conference calling, 43, 55
start-before-the-start activity planner, 100–103, 101f, 103f
status indicators, 49, 50, 107
stick figure introductions (activity), 103, 103f
Stone, Tom, 96, 96f
strategic plan, 9
strategy planner worksheet, evaluation, 193–194
strategy planning meetings, 29–32
Stroud, Katie, 87–90
subject matter experts (SMEs), 73
success, setting learners up for, 99
support materials, 72
surveys, 195–196, 201–202

T

teaching tools in the moment, 174
technology. *See also* platforms and platform tools
    about, 37
    audio, 40, 43–44, 55, 134
    blended learning and, 74
    engagement and, 147
    facilitator/producer requirements checklist, 58, 134
    hardware, 38–41, 39f, 134
    hosted *versus* on-site solutions, 53
    Internet bandwidth, 25, 40, 44–45, 45f
    IT department, partnering with, 47–48
    managing, 147
    participant requirements checklist, 59
    planning worksheet, 46
    request for proposal template, 56–57
    skills, learning, 135
    software, 41–42, 134, 137, 155
    tips, tools, and templates, 45–59
    traditional classroom *versus* virtual facilitation, 128
technology partners. *See* facilitators and producers
telephony, 43–44, 138
templates
    blended learning design, 77, 77f
    budget, 23
    design document, 80
    design process, 64
    4 Ts, 75
    hybrid program session planner, 91
    Level 1 surveys, 195–196
    meeting minutes and action items, 32
    participant roster, 180
    planning meeting agenda, 31
    post-pilot action tracker, 190
    project team charter and strategy, 33–34
    request for proposal (RFP), 56–57
    team charter and strategy, 33–34
    webcast session planner, 86

tests and quizzes tool, 49, 50
togetherness requirements, 74
traditional classroom *versus* virtual facilitation, 128
trainers. *See* facilitators and producers
trends
    about, 207
    massive open online courses, 207–208
    metrics, 210
    microbursts, 209
    mobile devices, 208
    modern learners, 209–210
    virtual training, 2–3
trivia questions, 108
troubleshooting guide for participant connections, 179
typing skills, 155

U

unexpected, responding to, 152
upskilling, 70, 126, 128

V

virtual classroom platforms. *See* platforms and platform tools
virtual learning prerequisite program, 171
virtual trainers. *See* facilitators and producers
virtual training. *See also specific topics*
    appropriateness of, 11
    components, 7f, 72
    defining, 7–8, 17–20
    perceptions about, 119
    trends, 2–3, 207–211
Virtual Training Guidebook, The (Huggett), 38, 146–147,
    207, 208, 209
visual aids, 69, 72
vocal warm-up exercises, 156
voice, using, 147
VoIP, 43–44, 55
Volvo Trucks, 9

W

webcams, 40–41, 157–158, 157f
webcasts
    agenda, sample, 85–86
    components, 7f
    designing for, 85–86
    interactivity, 7f, 118
    participants, number of, 7f
    platform tools for, 50
    purpose of, 95
webinars, 7f
welcome message from senior leader, 106
what's outside your window? (activity), 108
whiteboards
    about, 50
    activity idea for, 107
    closing activity ideas, 111, 112f
    description and sample use, 49
    insights, sharing, 111, 112f
    plus/minus, 197, 197f

wired/wireless headsets, 40
worksheets
   activities, questions to ask when creating, 113
   audio options, 55
   benefit-cost analysis, 24–25
   brainstorming, 15
   evaluation strategy planner, 193–194
   goal-planning, 14
   IT department, partnering with, 48
   opening activity planner, 105
   participants, getting to know, 144
   sequencing activities, 114–115
   start-before-the-start activity planner, 102
   technology planning, 46
workspace, setting up, 136, 136f
write space on slides, 117

Y

yoga pose, chair, 108